CROCKERY COOKERY

by Mable Hoffman

CROCKERY COOKERY

Introduction 3
Slow cooking is different, learn more
about it.
Menu Planning Guide 4
What to fix in the time you have.
Use & Care 5
Hints to let you get the utmost
use and life from your slow cooker.
Metric Conversion Chart &
    Table of Measurements 9
Simple conversions to fit these
recipes to the Metric System.
Consumers' Guide 10
Pots described with temperature
charts and details on how these
recipes work with each pot. Cleaning
hints.
Beef 28
Stretch your budget with cheap cuts
that turn out gourmet tender.
Other Meats 67
Pork & lamb turn out superbly in
your slow pot.
Poultry 80
Chicken, turkey and duck simmer to
delightful tastiness.
Vegetables 99
Require longer to cook than you
might think.
Appetizers & Beverages 111
Serve your party from your slow-
cooking pot.
Soups & Sandwiches 122
Hearty soups and delicious sandwiches
for company or family.
Main Dishes 136
One-dish meals—add a salad and des-
sert and do the rest in the pot.
Beans 142
New and old ways to fix 'em—all
delicious!
Breads & Cakes 150
Bake in a crockery pot? Absolutely!
Fruits & Desserts 161
Grandmother's desserts come to life
again to treat your family and friends.
Index 174
Spice Chart 176

Recipes Developed
    and Tested: Mable Hoffman
Co-Author: Howard Fisher
Managing Editor: Carl Shipman
Editors: Grace Williams
                     Bill Fisher
                     Helen Fisher
                     Howard Fisher
                     Karen Fisher
Food Photography: Naurice Koonce
Book Design: Josh Young
Book Assembly: Nancy Fisher
Typesetting: Ellen L. Duerr
Publisher: Bill Fisher

Library of Congress Cataloging in
    Publication Data

Hoffman, Mable, 1922—
    Crockery cookery.

Includes index.
    1. Cookery. 2. Casserole receipts.
I. Title.
TX652.H59   641.5   74-30823
ISBN 0-912656-44-1
ISBN 0-912656-43-3 pbk.

Paperback,
    ISBN: 0-912656-43-3
Hardcover,
    ISBN: 0-912656-44-1
Library of Congress Catalog
    Card No. 74-30823
H. P. Book No. 43, Paperback
H. P. Book No. 44, Hardcover
© 1975 Printed in U.S.A. 2-75
H. P. Books, P. O. Box 5367
Tucson, AZ 85703
602/888-2150

INTRODUCTION

Welcome to good eating! Slow cooking is the secret of good cooks the world over. With a modern electric slow-cooking pot, you can enjoy delicious simmered-in flavors of some of the world's best dishes without the time-consuming necessity of constant attention.

You can go to work or spend a day at leisurely shopping while your slow-cooking pot gently mingles flavors and spices—and retains many vitamins high temperatures destroy. You return home to a piping-hot dinner that's ready to serve. It doesn't matter even if you're an hour or two late. It won't burn or taste overcooked. Dinner is ready when you are!

Superb and truly nourishing meals can be prepared with inexpensive meats because slow cooking tenderizes in a special way that broiling or frying just can't duplicate. Meats are juicy and never cooked dry because slow-cooking pots seal in the moisture. Farm-kitchen favorites such as stews and hearty soups simmer to perfection with this new but old way to cook.

Gourmet foods are just as easy with the recipes in this book—such as *Teriyaki Steak, Chicken Marengo, Burgundy Duckling* and *Rhineland Sweet-Sour Cabbage.*

Electric slow-cooking pots are popular because they save time, money and energy. On a low setting, you'll be cooking with less energy than a 100-watt bulb. You can cook all day for only a few pennies—far less than the cost of cooking the same meal on your kitchen stove. You will also find that the slow-cooking pot does not make your kitchen hot in the summertime.

Gourmet foods, economy and the luxury of time are all yours with this new way of electric slow cooking.

Slow cooking is different and requires special recipes. The recipes in this book were developed specifically for electric slow-cooking pots. Every recipe has been tested and re-tested to bring you success with each meal you prepare.

The recipes are arranged in categories: Beef, poultry, vegetables, soups, desserts, etc. Within each group you will find a tantalizing variety so you can plan and serve meals to fit your tastes and preferences.

As you become familiar with this cooking method, you will see how your slow-cooking pot invites culinary creativity. Consider these recipes as basic and add a little pinch of your own ingenuity to the pot.

You'll find slow cooking makes good eating!

MENU PLANNING GUIDE

The most obvious use for your slow-cooking pot is to start a one-pot meal, go to work and return home to a ready-to-serve dinner. But this is just the beginning of slow-cooking convenience! Your slow-cooking pot has eliminated a lot of preparation time. Why not use that extra time to prepare a special dessert or side dish?

Slow-cookers are also convenient for foods which need less than a full day to cook. Whatever your activities, this book has recipes to complement *your* day. Prepare company dinner or a hot lunch, after-game snacks or hearty soups.

Here are a variety of recipes with different cooking times and ideas to adapt your slow-cooking pot to your lifestyle. Which of these situations fits you?

2-4 HOURS COOKING TIME

Invite guests over for the evening or bring home friends from a tennis match or committee meeting. Treat them to some of these piping-hot, slow-cooked specialties. They're sure to be a hit.

> *Hot Buttered Punch*
> *Hot Wine Cranberry Punch*
> *Sloppy Joes or Sloppy Janes*
> *All-American Snack*

3-4 HOURS COOKING TIME

Football and basketball seasons are great times for after-the-game parties. Cold weather and the excitement of a good game contribute to big appetites, so invite your friends over for hot punch and a crunchy snack.

Morning of Game—Mix together all ingredients of *All-American Snack* and cook as directed. Wash slow-cooking pot. One hour before game place ingredients for *Hot Buttered Punch* in slow-cooking pot, start on LOW. Spread cooled *All-American Snack* on baking sheet, ready to warm in the oven when you return. Now go and have a good time!

After the Game—Warm snack in 350°F. oven for 15 minutes; serve from nut dishes. Ladle punch into mugs, dot with butter and cinnamon sticks; serve while waiting for snack to heat.

Armchair fans need not miss out on this one—just have everything ready when the game starts.

4-5 HOURS COOKING TIME

Chicken in the freezer? Why not try a new recipe? *Chicken Breasts, Saltimbocca Style* is delicious, and you'll be free to do as you please for the rest of the day.

Night Before—Put chicken breasts out to thaw.

Morning of Dinner—Bone chicken breasts. Follow recipe directions and while chicken is chilling, you can get ready for a day's outing.

Brown chicken and place in slow-cooking pot with other ingredients, turn it on and off you go! If you'll be gone longer than the cooking time, turn the pot on with a timer.

When you come home, add the finishing touches to the chicken and serve with hot rice and applesauce. *Spicy Applesauce* is especially good with chicken. You'll have a dinner sure to please.

4-6 HOURS COOKING TIME

Be everyone's favorite luncheon and party host by serving delightful menus with ease. Don't worry about mid-day entertaining—just serve one of these easy-to-prepare treats:

> *Mock Chili Relleno*
> *Kowloon Chicken*
> *Turkey Loaf*
> *Bishop's Wine*
> *Short-Cut Chili Con Carne*

6-8 HOURS COOKING TIME

You can serve an exquisite company dinner with ease even after shopping or working all day. Just decide what to fix early enough to let meat thaw, start your dinner and be on your way. Supplement elegant main dishes with convenience foods, and you'll serve a memorable dinner with ease and confidence. For starters:

> *Beef Burgundy*
> *Barbecued Spare Ribs*
> *Chicken Breasts, Saltimbocca Style*
> *Chicken Parmigiana*

Here's how to do it with *Teriyaki Steak*. If the meat you have is still frozen, or only partially thawed, don't worry. Frozen meat is easier to cut into thin strips for *Teriyaki Steak*. Place meat and remaining ingredients in slow-cooking pot, set to cook for six hours and enjoy your day.

Round out your dinner menu with frozen Chinese vegetables, instant rice and a green salad with your favorite dressing. Last minute preparations take only 20 to 25 minutes.

Serve orange sherbet and almond cookies for dessert.

7-8 HOURS COOKING TIME

This elegant company dinner is designed especially for the person who works full-time, yet enjoys entertaining dinner guests during the week. You will need only 15-20 minutes to stuff the chicken and start it cooking, and even less time for last-minute preparation of salad, relish tray and rolls. Your guests will marvel at your organization, and you can serve a dinner to be proud of.

> *Busy Woman's Roast Chicken,*
> served with
> *Salad with Bleu Cheese Dressing*
> *Relish Tray—olives, celery, or*
> *canned fruits*
> *Rolls and Butter—Refrigerator or*
> *Brown n' Serve*
> *Coffee-Tea*
> *1-2-3 Jello*
> *Short-Cut Fruitcake (optional)*

Two Days Before—Prepare *Short-Cut Fruitcake.*

Night Before—If chicken is frozen, put out to thaw. Prepare dressing mix, let cool; refrigerate. Peel and cut carrots into 2-inch pieces, 1/2-inch thick. Place in small amount of water; boil 5 minutes. Drain; cool; refrigerate. Prepare *Jello* as directed, cover dishes with plastic wrap and refrigerate. To prepare *Bleu Cheese Dressing:* Break 4 oz. Danish bleu cheese into small pieces with fork, add 1 pint sour cream, 2 tbs mayonnaise, and 1 1/2 tsp. lemon pepper seasoning. Mix well and refrigerate.

Approximate preparation time is one hour.

Morning of Dinner—Rinse and dry chicken; season cavity with salt and pepper. Stuff with cold dressing; lightly salt and pepper chicken. Place carrots in bottom of slow-cooking pot. Add stuffed and trussed chicken. Attach timer; set for 7 hours cooking time.

Fifteen minutes before serving, remove chicken from pot, place in roasting pan;

brown in 400°F. oven. Prepare salad and relish tray. Heat rolls in oven.

There you have it! A full company dinner with less work than you'd dreamed possible . . . and no worries!

8-10 HOURS COOKING TIME

Now that the do-it-yourself movement is in full swing, why not invite friends over to help with that special painting job? When they're all finished, serve them the best-tasting *Old Fashioned Beef Stew* they've had in years.

Night Before—Cut up and brown meat; drain excess fat; refrigerate. Clean and chop all vegetables, cover with plastic wrap. Refrigerate.

That Morning—Place all ingredients in slow-cooking pot, turn on LOW, cover and forget it. While dinner cooks, you'll be painting away; your helpers won't have to run to the kitchen to ask what to do next.

Serve something easy for lunch, like instant soup and sandwiches (also prepared the night before).

When the painting is done, make the gravy and set the table while everyone is cleaning up. A sure hit!

8-10 HOURS COOKING TIME

Working people know better than anyone else how hard it is to cook after working all day. You are the people we have written this book for! Start nutritious, taste-tempting meals in the morning, when you're full of energy, then sit down and RELAX when you get home; dinner will be ready! You may find yourself eating better than you have in years by using these energy and time-saving recipes. Here are just a few:

> *Spicy Wine Pot Roast*
> *Gourmet Leg of Lamb*
> *Stuffed Flank Steak*
> *Chinese Style Country Ribs*

Use your imagination to create your own menus. Use similar recipes and cooking times in *Crockery Cookery* to help you adapt your own favorite recipes. Be adventurous; try out your own ideas and substitute ingredients to fit your taste.

Don't limit yourself to recipes that take a certain amount of time. A timer allows you to prepare any recipe. With planning, you can adapt any recipe in this book to your particular needs. And don't hesitate to combine ideas from two recipes to create your own new recipes.

USE & CARE

YOUR SLOW-COOKING POT

An electric slow-cooking pot is a new type of household appliance offering convenience and capability. As with any new appliance, there are some things to learn about its use and care. These are discussed in this chapter.

SLOW COOKING

Low temperature is the success factor in slow cooking. Low heat and long cooking times retain more vitamins and help simmer flavor into food. It is best to use recipe times suggested in this book; however, if you cook longer, don't worry. Your food will not burn because it does not overheat.

LEAVE IT ALONE

The advantage of slow cooking is to *set it and forget it* because there is no need to tend the pot. Don't hesitate to leave your house to do what you want.

STIRRING

Stirring is not required for recipes in this book or for slow cooking in general. Basting and brushing are needed for some recipes.

KEEP IT COVERED

Leave the lid on. There is no need to keep looking at food as it simmers in a slow-cooking pot. Steam and nutrients are trapped on the lid, condensed and returned to the cooking pot. The steam atmosphere above the food helps cook from the top. Every time you take the lid off, the pot loses steam. After you put the lid back on, it takes 15 to 20 minutes to regain the lost steam and temperature. Thus, taking the lid off means longer cooking times. *Never* remove the lid during the first two hours when *baking* breads or cakes.

COOKING TIMES

Consult the Consumers' Guide chapter for cooking time variations for your par-

Steam and vitamins condense on the lid and return to the pot to keep food moist and nutritious even after cooking many hours.

ticular brand of slow-cooking pot. Until you become familiar with your slow cooker, follow the suggested times. If you prefer softer vegetables or more well-done meat, cook longer than the indicated times.

Generally one hour on HIGH is equal to two hours on LOW.

HIGH—ALTITUDE COOKING

Allow more time than given in the recipe at high altitudes (over 4,000 feet). Whether you are using a slow-cooking pot, stove or oven, food takes longer to cook at high altitudes.

Beans take about double the time given in the recipe. To reduce cooking time for beans, cover with water, bring to boil in pan on stove, simmer for two minutes. Let cool one hour. Soak overnight. Return beans to slow cooker and proceed with the recipe.

Baking also requires longer cooking times. See direction on cake mix to adjust for high altitude. Be sure to bake on HIGH.

TEMPERATURES

Recipes in this book refer to two temperature settings, LOW and HIGH. LOW is 200°F. (93°C.) and HIGH is 300°F. (149°C.). Food in the pot seldom gets hotter than 212°F. (100°C.), as discussed on page 10.

MINIMUM LOW TEMPERATURE

Because slow cooking uses very low temperatures, it is important that all food inside the pot is hot enough to cook properly and avoid food spoilage. A minimum safe temperature for food while cooking is 180°F. (82°C.). Some adjustable heat controls have low-temperature settings which should not be used for cooking. They are too cool to cook food safely.

BROWNING UNIT

Some recipes refer to slow-cooking with browning units, an extra-high setting of 350°F.-450°F. (175°C.-230°C.) for browning meat quickly before slow cooking. If you brown or heat meat quickly, remember to turn the control knob back to the proper slow-cook setting before leaving the pot unattended. Some slow-cooking pots with this feature include: Corning, Farberware, Nesco, Oster and Regal.

TEMPERATURE SWITCHES

Some slow-cooking pots have a three-position switch, OFF-LOW-HIGH. The switch snaps into the desired position as you turn it. You must snap this switch to LOW or HIGH to cook, not in between.

TEMPERATURE CONTROL UNITS

Other slow-cooking pots have a continuously adjustable thermostatic-heat-control unit to keep the temperature within a few degrees or at the same temperature for hours. The Slow-Cooking Pot chapter gives time and temperature suggestions for your particular brand.

Here is the right way to use a heat-control unit if it is a removable one:

1. Insert the control all the way into the pot.
2. Connect the cord to 120-volt AC outlet.
3. Turn control to desired setting.

To disconnect, turn control to OFF and remove the plug from wall outlet. The pot and heat-control housing will be hot after use. If you must remove the heat control before the pot is cool, use a pot holder. Do not touch the metal themostat probe and do not let the probe come into contact with other materials.

To clean, wipe with a damp cloth. *Do not immerse any electric control unit in water.*

PILOT LIGHT

Thermostatic-heat-control units have a pilot light which glows when heating (using electricity) and is off when the pot reaches the desired temperature.

The pilot light turns on and off indicating the temperature is being maintained within a narrow range by switching electricity on and off to the heating unit.

TIMED COOKING

Take complete advantage of the convenience of your slow-cooking pot by using a timer or timed electrical outlet to turn the pot on while you are away.

A timer allows you to prepare recipes that cook in less time than you will be away *and* those you never seem to have enough time to cook—such as squash or roasted chicken. You can have a hot—not burned—dinner when you arrive home.

To use a timer with a slow-cooking pot, *plan for the timer to turn it* ON, *not* OFF. Subtract the recipe cooking time from your expected return time. Set the timer to turn your pot on at this time.

TIMED RECEPTACLE

Many electric ranges have timed receptacles. These are especially convenient but make sure yours works like you think it does before you gamble your dinner on it. To test, plug in an appliance and set the timer to turn on in a short time. Now, turn the appliance ON. If the timed receptacle works, your appliance will start in a few minutes.

TIMERS

If you don't have a timed receptacle, buy an appliance timer. They range in price from $6 to $25. This is the same kind of timer that turns on your house lights to foil burglars while you are away. In addition, you can use it to turn on a variety of appliances, even your coffee pot before you get up in the morning.

The most practical electric timers offer a receptacle for your appliance cord, ON and OFF settings, and wattage ratings high enough for many household appliances. Intermatic, GE and others make the kind you need.

FROZEN FOODS

Frozen foods should be thawed before placing them in your slow cooker. Some glass-lined or metal cooking surface pots (bare-metal, Teflon or porcelainized) can be used with foods which are still frozen. Several extra hours must be added to the

This switch snaps into the OFF, LOW or HI setting. Do not set the switch between OFF and LOW or LOW and HI because the pot will not heat. There are no "in-between" settings.

cooking time to compensate for the time required for the food to thaw before cooking actually begins. I wouldn't consider doing this with a crockery-lined pot or a crockery pot because I think you'd probably break the crockery.

In some cases, I have recommended using partially thawed (still frosty on the inside) vegetables in stews and soups. This works fine and will not require modifying the times I have given in the recipes.

SPICES

Because little evaporation takes place when cooking with your slow cooker, there are more juices when you finish than you would have with other cooking methods. For this reason you may want to adjust the amount of spices you use in my recipes so they will suit your taste.

FOIL SPEEDS COOKING

You can decrease cooking times a bit by using a piece of aluminum foil on top of the contents or between the lid and the pot. The foil reflects heat back into the food—heat which would otherwise be lost through the lid. This trick can help speed up cooking in a cooker which cooks at lower temperatures than I used for my recipe testing. The temperature charts in the cooker description section show which ones give temperatures which I felt were on the low side of what was needed.

MEAT RACK

A metal meat rack or trivet will keep a roast out of juices and fats in the bottom

Different heat control units: Three units on left, Farberware, Oster and Sunbeam, are thermostatically controlled—you select the desired temperature. The Crock-Pot control at right is a switch with distinct OFF, LOW or HI positions.

This Intermatic timer plugs into a kitchen receptacle. Your appliance plugs in at the bottom.

These Intermatic timers are designed to use with household appliances when you need extra cord length. Model at left has standard ON-OFF settings. Multi-program timer at right has tab inserts to turn power ON and OFF more than once during 24 hours. A great burglar deterrent when used with a lamp.

of the cook pot and prevents the meat from sticking to the bottom. Use a meat rack *only* when the recipes say to; it is not necessary or useful for all meats. It is most useful for fatty meats or roasts which produce a lot of grease while cooking.

BAKING PANS AND DISHES

You can bake without modifying the recipes in this book in these brands of slow-cooking pots: Corning, Cornwall 4-quart (not tray model), Dominion, Empire, Grandinetti, Hamilton Beach, Penneys, Regal Poly Pot, Reliable Crockery Slow Cooker, Rival, Sears 4-quart (not tray model), Sunbeam, Van Wyck Sim·R·Pot, Wards Crockery Slow Cooker, Wear·Ever Pokey·Pot. West Bend 4-quart Slo-Cooker, Lazy Day Slo-Cooker and Slo-Cooker Plus.

With special care you can also bake in these pots: Farberware, Nesco, Oster, Presto and Regal Pot O'Plenty. These slow-cooking pots are trickier to bake in because they are basically frypans or deep fryers; they heat very quickly and water evaporates more rapidly. Check water once or twice in the middle of baking. If it has evaporated, add more water.

Do not try to bake in the Cornwall tray model or the Sears tray model unless you use water. If all the water evaporates, they will overheat and break. These pots cannot be used dry.

Baking requires a separate pan inside your slow-cooking pot. The Breads and Cakes chapter shows you how to use coffee cans, ring molds, tube pans and souffle dishes.

LIDS AND HANDLES

Become familiar with your pot to prevent a burned hand or spill. Lids are glass, plastic or metal. The handle on a glass or metal lid gets hot enough so you'll need a pot holder. Keep the glass handle clean and free of oil so it won't slip out of your grasp.

Pot handles are usually located near the top of the pot. This is the safest location. Handles near the bottom of the pot make the pot unwieldy to handle. Most handles are safe to use but some are dangerously close to the heated exterior surface. Check whether you are going to get burned before you put your hand anywhere on the pot; use pot holders to be safe.

CORDS

Most slow-cooking pots come with a short cord. This is a safety precaution to eliminate long, dangerous dangling cords that can be pulled on by children or tripped over. Many pots have the cord attached which means the cooking pot is non-immersible. You can eliminate some of the nuisance of a dangling cord while washing and handling. Wrap up the cord as short as practical and tie with a rubber band or plastic tie. This helps keep the cord from dangling around the sink and getting wet or in the way.

EXTENSION CORDS

Extension cords may be used with most slow-cooking pots if you exercise care. The marked electrical rating of an extension cord should be at least as great

as the electrical rating of the appliance— at least 15 amperes. The longer cord should be arranged so that it will not drape over the counter or table top where it can be pulled on by children or tripped over. If the extension cord gets warm or hot, it is not adequate and should not be used.

A SAFE POT

Place your pot on a flat, level surface. Put it where it cannot be accidentally moved, touched or tipped over by guests or children. Place the cord so it cannot be entangled and does not touch the hot surface of the pot.

Some slow-cooking pots are insulated so the outside surface does not get very hot. In this category are the 4 1/2-quart Crock-Pot, Regal Pot O'Plenty and Regal Poly Pot. You can touch these models after a day's cooking and not get burned; even the bottom is only warm. The outside surfaces of some of the other slow-cooking pots will burn you, so be careful. Watch that your children don't try to touch the pot.

BEFORE YOU START COOKING

Wash the inside of your new pot in soapy water. Do not immerse the pot in water unless it has a separate heating unit. Crockery, Teflon, Teflon II, aluminum, porcelain, stainless steel and glass may have a manufacturer's finishing coating you can't see and don't want in your food. Washing removes it.

A meat rack is used in some recipes to keep meat out of fatty juices. It is not used or necessary to cook all meats. Use only when directed.

Glass lids often get very hot. Use a pot holder to be safe.

If you don't have a meat rack, use a trivet. Any style will do. A trivet is often suggested in the Breads and Cakes chapter.

Teflon, aluminum or stainless steel pots should be seasoned to reduce the chance of sticking and protect the cooking surface. To season your pot, rub the inside surface lightly with cooking oil or shortening. Remove the excess with a paper towel.

HOW TO CLEAN YOUR SLOW COOKER

Preventive maintenance and care will keep your pot looking new. Don't allow food stains to burn into the finish. Soak the inside of the pot with warm soapy water to loosen food, then scrub lightly with a plastic or nylon pad. Rinse well and dry.

Different brands of slow cookers use different materials. Here are tips on the cleaning and caring for the various surfaces.

CROCKERY

Crockery is a term for several varieties of stoneware and earthenware. Slow-cooking crockery pots are fired at high temperatures to make the pot and glazed surface non-porous and safe for cooking. Crockery pots should be washed soon after using. If your crockery liner is removable from the heating unit, it can be dishwasher cleaned or washed as you would any other pot or pan. If the crockery portion is not removable, *do not immerse the entire unit in water.* Fill the pot with hot soapy water to loosen stubborn food. Use a plastic cleaning pad to remove residue. Do not use abrasive compounds like household cleansers or steel-wool soap pads.

If stains accumulate, remove them with a Teflon cleaner. Use three or four tablespoons of cleaner with enough hot water to cover the stain. Simmer one hour, rinse well and dry.

All crockery can be broken by a sharp blow so use special caution around the sink.

Crockery should not be exposed to *sudden* changes in temperature. Allow the pot to attain room temperature before heating. If the pot is hot, do not fill with cold water.

CAUTION: Do not scrape or scratch crockery to remove stubborn food. Food will stick at the scratch later. Instead, fill the pot with water and let it soak. Also, keep kitchen utensils out of the pot when cleaning up. A knife or handful of silverware can scratch the cooking surface. If the glaze on the cooking surface of the crockery pot should crack, get a new liner or crock. A crack in the glaze can trap food you can never clean out. This could be a place for bacteria to grow and you don't want that!

STAINLESS STEEL

Wash in hot soapy water. Remove food particles with a sponge, vegetable brush and scouring cleanser. You can use a steel-wool scouring pad for any additional cleaning. Do not use steel-wool cleaning pads on the polished outside of your pot. You will scratch the surface, and the mistake is nearly impossible to polish out. Rub the outside of your stainless steel pot with a sponge, cloth or plastic cleaning pad. Rub in the direction of the polishing lines; dry thoroughly to prevent water spots.

If your pot is a stainless steel/aluminum base combination, as the Farberware Pot-

Pourri pans, use steel-wool pads to clean up the aluminum on the base.

PORCELAIN AND BAKED ENAMEL

Let pot cool completely before washing. Clean the pot and lid in hot soapy water, using a sponge, dish cloth or plastic pad. A non-abrasive cleaner such as *Bon Ami* may be used if necessary on the porcelain finish. Apply with a cloth or sponge, using a circular motion. DO NOT use a metal scouring pad or harsh scouring powder on the porcelain finish. After washing, rinse pot thoroughly and dry. If detergent is not entirely rinsed off, it can result in stained areas when re-heated.

ALUMINUM

Wash pot in hot soapy water. Stubborn food or stains should be soaked and scrubbed off with a plastic or nylon scouring pad. If food is very stubborn, use steel wool pads.

In the event the aluminum cooking surface discolors, follow the stain removal procedure outlined for Teflon, using *Dip It.* Re-season pot after cleaning. Additional usage may cause a white mineral film to form on the cooking surface. Wipe away with vinegar or lemon juice. Re-season pot.

On aluminum slow-cooking pots with a non-stick coating such as the Oster Super Pot, the aluminum base may be cleaned with a commercial degreaser, but be sure not to get the cleaner on the cooking surface. Steel-wool cleaning pads will also help clean up the base.

Many slow-cooking pots have metal sides that get very hot while cooking. Be careful to avoid touching the hot pot with your hands or arms.

On pots with attached cords, keep the cord wrapped up with a rubber band or plastic tie. It will be easier to handle, especially when cleaning.

Slow-cooking pots with attached cords cannot be immersed. To clean, place pot in empty sink, then fill with warm soapy water. Wash and pour out water. Rinse out inside of pot and dry.

CORNING WARE & GLASS LINERS

Corning Ware cookware is made of glass-ceramic material which absorbs heat rapidly and holds heat a long time. These qualities make it ideal for slow cooking.

Another special Corning Ware feature is its ability to withstand extreme temperatures and sudden temperature changes. You can take your Corning Ware directly from the freezer or refrigerator and place it on the heating surface.

Corning Ware is very easy to clean; these directions keep it looking and cooking like new.

Usually, you can remove food with hot soapy water and a dish cloth or plastic scouring pad. Do not use metal scouring pads, as these will scratch the ceramic glaze.

For burned-on food, soak pot in soapy water. Use cleanser or baking soda with a damp cloth.

When sugary or starchy foods stick to Corning Ware, soak or boil with baking soda (3 tbs. soda to 1 qt. water). For greasy foods, soak pot in ammonia and water. Use cleanser if necessary.

NO-STICK & TEFLON COATINGS

Wash with warm soapy water and dry thoroughly. No-Stick and Teflon surfaces are damaged by steel-wool scouring pads or abrasive kitchen cleansers. A plastic cleaning pad (nylon) can be used on stubborn food.

In time, these surfaces will discolor over the heating element. This is normal and will not affect anti-stick and easy-clean qualities. To reduce discoloration, thoroughly wash your pot after each use. When discoloration becomes noticeable,

you can remove it with special appliance stain removers like *Dip It*, available at your grocery store. Follow the manufacturer's instructions and wear gloves. Wipe off any remover that gets on the outside of your pot or pan; the solution may remove the baked enamel or porcelain finish. After removing stains, rinse thoroughly and dry. Re-season your pot by rubbing lightly with cooking oil.

CAUTION: Do not scrape or scratch Teflon or No-Stick finish to remove stubborn food. Food will stick at the scratch later. Instead set the pot to soak. Also, as good practice, keep your kitchen utensils out of the pot when cleaning up. A knife or handful of silverware can scratch the cooking surface.

Teflon II is now available in some pots. DuPont has improved the finish to last longer, clean easier and stain less.

METRIC CONVERSION CHART

Metric Units:

1 kilogram (kg)	= 1000 grams
1 gram (gm)	= 1000 milligrams
1 milligram (mg)	= 1000 micrograms (mcg)

Weight:

Metric		U.S. Avoirdupois
1 kilogram = 1000 gm		= 2.2 pounds
0.1 kilogram = 100 gm		= 3.52 ounces
0.454 kilogram = 454 gm		= 1.0 pound
0.028 kilogram = 28.4 gm		= 1.0 ounce

Volume, Liquid:

3.785 liters		= 1 gallon
1.000 liter = 1000 ml		= 1.06 quarts
0.946 liter = 946 ml		= 1 quart
0.473 liter = 473 ml		= 1 pint
0.227 liter = 227 ml		= 1 cup
0.014 liter = 14.2 ml		= 1 tablespoon
	4.7 ml	= 1 teaspoon

Weight per Volume of Water:

1 liter	= 1 kg	
1 milliliter	= 1 gm	= 1 cubic centimeter
1 quart	= 946 gm	
1 cup	= 227 gm	= 8 ounces

TABLE OF MEASUREMENTS

3 teaspoons	=	1 tablespoon
16 tablespoons	=	1 cup
2 cups	=	1 pint
2 pints	=	1 quart
4 quarts	=	1 gallon
8 fluid ounces	=	1 cup
1 fluid ounce	=	2 tablespoons
16 ounces	=	1 pound
4 tablespoons	=	1/4 cup
8 tablespoons	=	1/2 cup
dash	=	less than 1/8 teaspoon

CONSUMERS' GUIDE TO SLOW-COOKING POTS

There is a particular slow-cooking pot to suit your needs. Some are designed soley for slow cooking—others are also frypans or deep fryers. Your choice of a slow-cooking pot will depend on the appliances you already have and use, and the size recipes you prepare.

Each brand has different capacity, shape, cooking surface, outside finish, handles, cord and temperature settings.

This chapter tells you things you need to know about each slow cooker, such as special handling hints so you don't get burned. Here are instructions for temperature control settings and times to match recipes in this book for each cooker. Special temperature charts show how each pot heats. And, there are clean-up hints, too!

These manufacturers have registered trademarks and product names referred to in *Crockery Cookery*.

Corning Electromatic
Corning Ware
Cornwall Crockery Cooker
Dobie
Dominion Crock-A-Dial & Crock-A-Dial II
DuPont Teflon and Teflon II
Empire Easy Meal
Farberware Pot-Pourri
General Electric Lexan
Grandinetti All American Crockery Casserole
Grandinetti All American Crockery Cook Pot
Hamilton Beach Continental Cooker, Crock-Watcher, Simmer-On
Intermatic Time-All
K-Mart LaCuisine Sim·R·Pot
Nesco Pot Luck
Oster Super Pot
Penneys Slow Cooker/Fryer
Penneys Slow Crockery Cooker
Presto Slow Cookers
Regal Mardi Gras Pot O'Plenty
Regal Poly Pot
Reliable Crockery Slow Cooker
Rival Crock-Pot
Robeson Sim·R·Pot
Scotch-Brite
Sears/Simpson Crockery Cooker
Sunbeam Crocker Cooker Fryer & Crocker Frypan
Van Wyck Sim·R·Ware
Van Wyck Sim·R·Pot
Wards Crockery Slow Cooker
Wear·Ever Pokey·Pot
West Bend Colonial Crock Slo-Cooker
West Bend Beans 'N Stuff Slo-Cooker
West Bend 4 Qt. Slo-Cooker
West Bend Lazy Day Slo-Cooker
West Bend Slo-Cooker Plus

Co-author Howard Fisher made the temperature tests. Heating was measured at each of the control settings. Manufacturers do change specifications from time to time—and not all pots of the same model are identical. Your pot may cook slower or faster than we say it will in the Temperature & Recipe Times descriptions. Your pot will probably perform very closely to the temperatures shown.

HOW TO READ TEMPERATURE CHARTS

The wide yellow bands in each chart represent the recipe HIGH and LOW temperature curves for comparison with all pots.

Red lines show the temperatures attained at each pot setting shown. Note the temperature lines for many pots exceed 300°F. *Food actually never gets this hot in your pot.* Cooking oil was used in one pot of each type to measure temperatures beyond the boiling point of water so you could see the relative heating characteristics for all the pots we tested.

A normal cooking mixture of meat, vegetables and liquid does not heat more than a few degrees above the boiling point of water (212°F. or 100°C.). Steam generated from the hot water condenses on the lid and drips down the sides of the crock to cool the pot and cooking mixture while maintaining a near-boiling temperature. Oil does not provide this cooling action, so our charts show higher temperatures.

Pot capacities are important when considering the relative temperatures of two pots. For instance, the 5 1/2-quart Reliable or 5 1/2-quart Wards and 8-quart Cornwall are designed to cook large quantities of food. Their higher wattage brings a large amount of ingredients to the proper cooking temperature and holds the temperature. To use our recipes with one of the large-capacity pots, reduce recipe times or double the recipe quantities. Then the recipe times and temperature settings will work fine.

2 1/2 quart

Corning Electromatic Table Range

You can slow cook with this unit. A separate Corning Ware casserole holds the food and rests on the Corning Ware cooking surface. The cord is detachable.

Temperature & Recipe Times—The variable temperature control has settings from 200°F. to 500°F. For the recipes in this book, set the temperature to 240°F. for LOW and 350°F. for HIGH. Use times provided in the recipes.

Cleaning—Do not immerse heating unit in water. Clean cooking surface with baking soda or other mild cleaner. Wipe wood grain and metal trim with a sudsy paper towel. The Use and Care chapter tells how to clean Corning Ware.

2 1/2-quart Casserole—Usable capacity is 1 3/4 quarts.
4 1/2-quart Dutch Oven & Rack—Usable capacity of this casserole is 3 1/2 quarts.

Cornwall 4-quart Crockery Cooker

Usable capacity is 3 1/2 quarts. This crockery pot has a painted-metal outside finish with attached cord. The lid is glass. The outside of the pot and the lid get very hot so use a pot holder to remove the lid and pick up the pot only by the handles. This cooker heats from the sides to provide even heat distribution from top to bottom.

Temperature & Recipe Times—The temperature switch has two positions: MED and HI. For recipes in this book MED should be used whenever LOW is called for . Use HI for HIGH settings. Use the times provided in the recipes.

Cleaning—Do not immerse to clean. Fill empty pot with water to soak off stubborn food. Use and Care chapter tells how to clean crockery. Wipe off outside of cooker with a damp cloth.

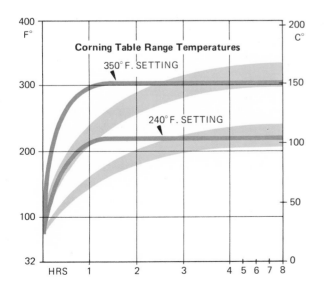

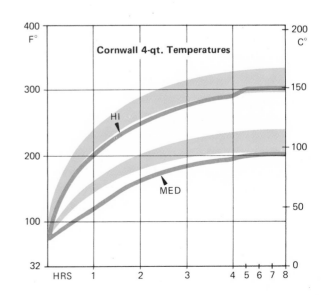

2 1/2 quart

4 1/2 quart

Cornwall Tray Model Crockery Cookers

These cookers differ from the previously discussed self-contained units in that they have an electric heating base and a separate crockery pot with lid. Each size allows you to cook a different quantity of food. The painted rectangular heating base has wooden handles at each end. There is an attached cord. The pot sits in a shallow heating well in the center of the heating base.

The crockery pots are dishwasher and oven safe, but you should not place the pot on any stove burner because that will probably break the pot. Always put ingredients into the pot *before* placing it on the heating base. If the crockery has been in the refrigerator, allow it to warm up to room temperature before placing it on the heating base. Turn on the heating base only after the crockery pot with its contents has been placed in the heating well.

WARNING: There must be at least one cup of liquid in any recipe used in this pot. Do not let the pot operate dry for baking and do not let all of the liquid evaporate. This pot will overheat and probably break if the liquid is allowed to evaporate.

The heating base may be used to warm other pots and pans for keeping food warm, but do not use the base as a griddle. Because both the pot and the heating base become very hot, use a pot holder or mitts to remove the pot. Lift it only by the handles. Do not attempt to move the base without pot holders. There are wooden ends, but these offer little protection against getting burned by the hot heating base. The heating bases smoke at first because the protective coatings are burned off as the heating element warms up.

Temperature & Recipe Times—Set the 4 1/2- and 8-qt. temperature controls to 2 for LOW and 3 for HIGH to use with recipes in this book. Position 1 is too cool to cook food properly. It is only designed for warming. Use the times given in the recipes. See special temperature note for 2 1/2-quart model below.

Cleaning—Never immerse the heating base in water. Wipe it clean with a damp cloth after it is completely cool. The Use and Care chapter explains how to clean crockery.

2 1/2-quart—Usable capacity 2 quarts. This pot is suited for one or two people. For the 4 to 6 serving recipes in this book, use one-half the ingredients. Setting 3 on the temperature control is equal to LOW. Use those recipes which cook only on LOW because this pot will not attain a temperature equal to a HIGH setting on other pots.

4 1/2-quart—Usable capacity 3 quarts. Recipes serving 4 to 6 fit nicely.

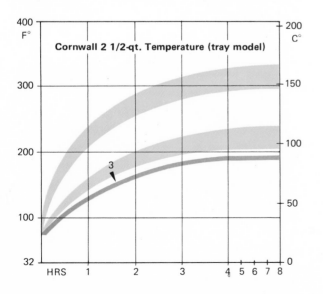

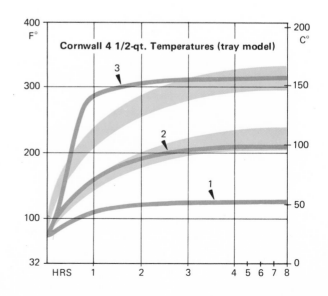

8 quart

8-quart—Usable capacity 7 quarts. Great for family-size or party meals. Double 4 to 6 serving recipes to take advantage of the capacity. If you do not double small recipe quantities, reduce cooking times.

Dominion Crock-A-Dial & Model 21-46

Usable capacity of these pots is 3 quarts. The liner in the *Crock-A-Dial* is crockery. *Crock-A-Dial II* has a glass liner. Sides are painted metal and the lids are glass. Cords are attached. Both units have heating coils around the liner to provide even top-to-bottom heating. The outside of the pot gets very hot. Use pot holders or mitts to remove the lid and pick up the pot only by the handles.

Temperature & Recipe Times—LOW COOK and HIGH COOK settings are somewhat lower than called for in the recipes and may require an added 2 hours or more on many recipes. The *Crock-A-Dial* has an AUTO-SHIFT setting which cooks for the first two hours at the high end of the LOW COOK setting, then switches to the LOW COOK setting. With AUTO-SHIFT, recipes calling for cooking on LOW should cook perfectly at the times specified in the recipes.

Cleaning—Do not immerse these pots. Wipe off the outside with a damp cloth. The Use and Care chapter tells how to clean crockery and glass.

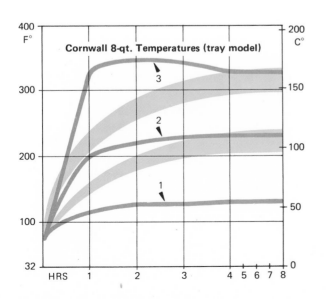

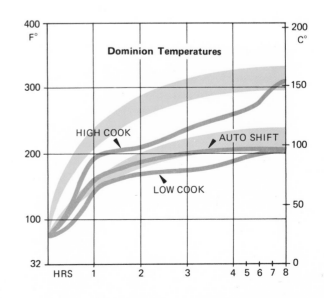

5 quart

Empire Easy Meal Slow Cooker

Usable capacity 2 1/2 quarts. This small-capacity slow cooker has a removable aluminum cooking well. The heating pot and lid are painted aluminum. The outside of the pot gets very hot, so use hot pads or mitts and always pick up the pot by the handles. The temperature control is close to hot metal. Be careful to avoid burning yourself. Food should only be placed in the removable cooking well insert.

Temperature & Recipe Times—The variable temperature dial does not have an OFF position. Unplug the detachable cord to turn the pot OFF. The HI setting heats very slowly, then gets very hot. LO is too low for slow cooking. For recipes in this book, set the temperature to MEDIUM for LOW. Use a one o'clock position for HIGH. This unit does not cook food as evenly as crockery-lined pots because the thin-walled aluminum cooking well does not heat uniformly. Cooking a small roast requires turning it over so it will cook evenly. Other foods may require occasional stirring. Use the recipe times provided.

Cleaning—The aluminum pot stains easily, but is easy to clean with *Dip It*. The heating pot is not immersible and should be cleaned with a damp cloth after the pot is unplugged and cool.

Farberware 3- and 5-quart Pot-Pourri

Usable capacity 2 1/2 and 4 quarts. These stainless-steel, all-purpose cookers are good for slow cooking, regular cooking and deep frying. The 5-quart model's high-domed lid allows extra height for cooking chickens or larger cuts of meat. The 3-qt. model has a long handle for one-hand carrying, but use both hands because a full pot is heavy. Carry these pots with the handles because all of the metal gets hot. The cord detaches with the temperature-control unit. Handy hint to prevent boil-overs: Fill the pot only 2/3 full of liquid.

Temperature & Recipe Times—Set the control at 200°F. for LOW and 300°F. for HIGH to fit the recipes. These pans attain selected temperatures within only a few minutes, so cooking times are shorter than given by the recipes. An 8 to 10 hour recipe should be reduced to a total time of 6 to 8 hours. Recipes with shorter times should be reduced by 1/4 to 1/2 of the recommended time.

Cleaning—These pots can be immersed for cleaning. The Use and Care chapter explains how to clean stainless steel. Do not immerse the temperature control unit. Wipe it clean with a damp cloth when it is cool.

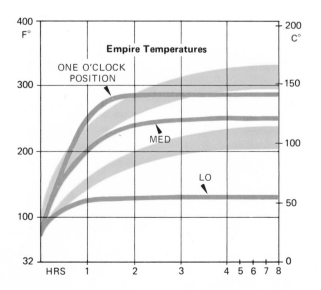

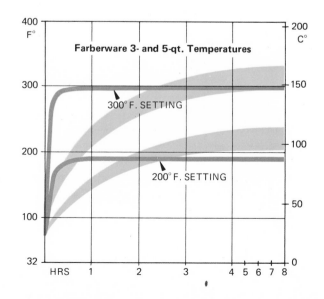

Grandinetti 4-quart All American Crockery Casserole
Usable capacity 3 1/2 quarts. The removable crockery casserole is an attractive serving dish which can be used at your dinner table. It is oven-proof and dishwasher safe, but you should not place the casserole on a stove burner or electric element because this will break the crockery. Do not turn pot ON before inserting casserole or you may break it. Lexan case and lid stay cool. The cord is attached. When you store food in the pot, allow the crockery to warm up to room temperature before re-heating or the bowl may break. To hasten warming, place the pot in warm—not hot—water.

The separate heating case heats evenly from the sides and should be used only to heat the casserole.

Temperature & Recipe Times—Make sure to turn the heat control switch to LOW or HIGH exactly. This pot cooks slower than the 3 1/2 and 5-quart Grandinetti models. Increase the maximum recipe times by at least two hours. Meat recipes requiring five hours or longer must be cooked at least an additional four hours on LOW, or two hours more on HIGH. If your food does not stand taller than the casserole lip, match recipe LOW times exactly by placing a piece of foil across the pot. Then replace the lid. This decreases the cooling atmosphere and speeds cooking. Do not use this method on HIGH.

Cleaning—The casserole can be put in the dishwasher. See the Use and Care chapter for details on cleaning crockery. Separate heating unit is not immersible. Wipe it off with a damp cloth if it becomes dirty.

Grandinetti 3 1/2-quart All American Crockery Cook Pot
Usable capacity 3 quarts. This popular pot fits most 4-5 serving recipes well. The pot has a painted-metal outside surface with a crockery liner and glass lid. The cord is attached. Do not touch the outside metal surface because it gets very hot. Plastic handles are on the sides. Hold onto them firmly. Heating elements wrapped around the pot provide even heating.

Temperature & Recipe Times—Make sure to turn the heat control switch to LOW or HIGH exactly. Use times provided in the recipes.

Cleaning—Because this pot is not immersible, fill it with warm soapy water to soak off stubborn food. Wipe off the outside with a damp cloth. The Use and Care chapter tells how to clean crockery.

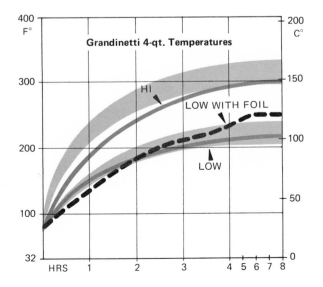

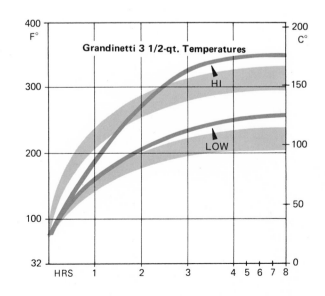

Grandinetti 5-quart All American Crockery Cook Pot

Usable capacity 4 quarts. This practical wide-mouth pot is ideal for roasts, chicken and large meals. Detachable cord includes temperature control. This pot has a painted-metal outside surface with a crockery liner. Do not touch the outside metal surface because it gets very hot. Lid stays cool because it is Lexan. Grasp the plastic handles on the sides firmly because they are slippery and sometimes hard to hold onto. Heating elements wrapped around the pot provide even heating of the contents.

Temperature & Recipe Times—Make sure the heating control switch is turned exactly to LOW or HIGH. The heat control unit must be pushed all the way into the pot. Turn OFF when inserting or removing the control unit. Use times provided in the recipes.

Cleaning—This pot is not immersible. Fill the empty pot with warm soapy water to soak off stubborn food. Wipe off the outside with a damp cloth. The Use and Care chapter tells how to clean crockery.

Hamilton Beach Continental Cooker, Crock-Watcher and Simmer-On

Usable capacity of these pots is 3 quarts. Liners for the *Crock-Watcher* and *Simmer-On* are crockery. *Continental Cooker* and *Simmer-On II* are glass-lined. Sides are painted metal and the lids are glass. Cords are attached. All models have heating coils around the liner to provide even top-to-bottom heating. The outside of the pots get very hot. Use pot holders or mitts to remove the lid and pick up the pot only by the handles.

Temperature & Recipe Times—HIGH COOK and LOW COOK settings are somewhat lower than called for in the recipes and may require an added 2 hours or more on many recipes. The *Continental Cooker* and *Crock-Watcher* have an added AUTO-SHIFT setting which cooks for the first two hours at the high end of the LOW COOK setting, then switches to the LOW COOK setting. With Auto-Shift, recipes calling for cooking on LOW should cook perfectly at the times specified in the recipes.

Cleaning—Do not immerse these pots. Wipe off the outside with a damp cloth. The Use and Care chapter tells how to clean crockery and glass.

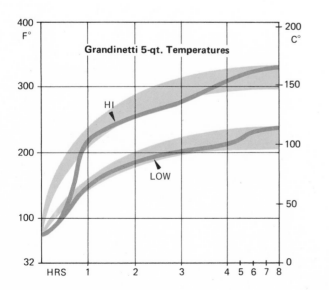

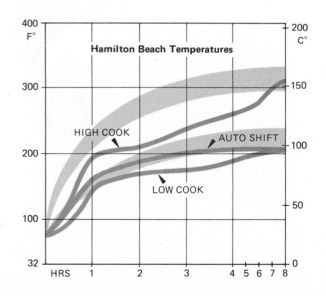

Nesco Pot Luck Cooker

Usable capacity 4 1/2 quarts. This cooker is fine for large meals and poultry. The painted all-metal pot has a removable metal liner with a porcelain-enamel cooking surface. It comes with a detachable cord and a meat rack. While this pot is sold as a slow-cooking unit, it is really a roaster with an added low-temperature setting. The high temperature range reaches 500°F. The primary item that separates this model from other slow cookers is two steam holes in the lid. These lose steam and liquid when used for slow cooking. If you intend to use one of these primarily for slow cooking, I suggest you close the lid holes with epoxy to avoid having to add more liquid at the start or while cooking so food does not dry out. The outside surface gets very hot and you must handle the unit by the handles and preferably with hot pads. Wraparound heating elements provide even heat from top to bottom.

Temperature & Recipe Times—Use the 200°F. LOW position for LOW. Use a 250°F. setting for HIGH. DO NOT USE THE 300°F. SETTING WITH THESE RECIPES. On an 8 to 10 hour recipe you must reduce cooking time to 6 to 8 hours. For shorter times, reduce time by 1/4 to 1/2.

Cleaning—The removable porcelain-enameled liner cleans easily with hot soapy water in the sink or dishwasher. Do not immerse the heating unit in water. Wipe it clean with a damp cloth.

Oster 8-quart Super Pot

Usable capacity 7 quarts. This versatile cooker/fryer has a wide temperature range and large capacity. It can be used for warming and serving, slow cooking, steaming, canning and deep frying. The deep pot will hold large roasts, chickens, and even a tube pan for baking. A trivet is included. The black Fluon non-stick cooking surface is similar to Teflon. The aluminum pot has a porcelain outer finish. The long, narrow handles are positioned so you can burn your hands unless you carefully place a pot holder between each hand and the outer surfaces of the pot. This pot is heavy when filled and you should cook and serve from it without moving the pot whenever possible. The cord is detachable.

Temperature & Recipe Times—This pot is also a deep fryer so it reaches selected temperatures in about 5 minutes—much quicker than crockery-lined pots. Recipe times must be reduced to avoid overcooking. On 8 to 10 hour recipes, reduce cooking time to 6 to 8 hours. For shorter times, reduce total time by 1/4 to 1/2. Set the temperature control to 200°F. for LOW and 300°F. for HIGH. Recipes in this book may be doubled to take full advantage of the size of this big pot.

Cleaning—This pot is especially convenient to clean because it is immersible. Oster recommends keeping it out of the dishwasher so the cooking surface will last longer.

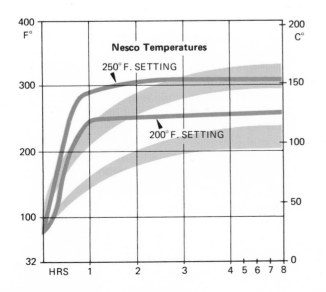

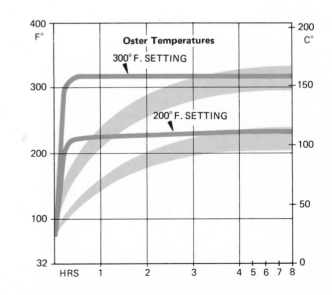

Penneys Slow Cooker/Fryer

Usable capacity 4 quarts. This unit cooks slowly and includes a removable crockery pot. The heavy-wall crock provides even heat distribution, even though heating is only from the bottom. A large lip on the pot makes it easy to handle and it is dishwasher safe and oven proof. This unit is both a cooker and a fryer, with high temperatures for deep frying. The cooker/fryer cooking surface is Teflon-coated.

Temperature & Recipe Times—For the recipes in this book, use 200°F. for LOW. Because there is no 200°F. marker on the dial, set it just to the left of the red CROCKERY band. For HIGH, set the dial between 325°F. and 350°F. Cooking times in the recipes work fine with this pot.

Cleaning—Remove the empty pot and fill with warm water to soak off stubborn food. The slow cooker/fryer heating portion does not get very dirty with slow cooking. Wiping with a damp cloth will usually clean off any spilled food. Do not immerse the cooker/fryer unit.

Penneys Slow Crockery Cooker

Usable capacity 3 quarts. Most 4-5 serving recipes fit this pot well. This pot has a crockery liner, glass lid and the cord is attached. Wraparound heating elements provide even cooking. The painted metal outside surface and lid get very hot and you should use hot pads and caution in handling them.

Temperature & Recipe Times—Temperature settings of LOW and HIGH are exactly as found in the recipes. Cooking times are the same as provided in the recipes. Turn the knob *exactly* to LOW or HIGH or the pot will not heat.

Cleaning—This pot is not immersible. Fill the empty pot with warm soapy water to soak off stubborn food. Follow the Use and Care chapter recommendations for cleaning crockery.

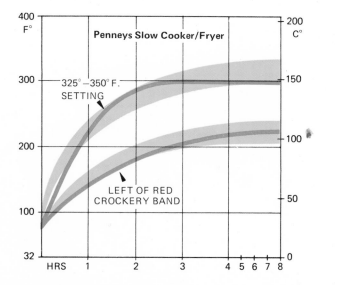

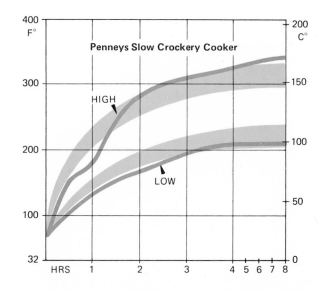

5 quart

Presto 2 3/4- and 5-quart Slow Cookers, Presto Create 'n Serve Pan, Presto Deep Fryer, and Sears Create 'n Serve Pan

Usable capacities are 2 quarts for all of the 2 3/4-qt. models, and 4 quarts for the 5-qt. slow cooker and deep fryer. These units have a non-stick cooking surface similar to Teflon. The lids are glass on the slow cookers and painted aluminum on the Create 'n Serve Pans and Deep Fryers. The 5-qt. models are the same unit with several additional inches of depth. These pots stand solidly and the handles are conveniently at the top of the pot. The glass lid gets hot and it also tends to slide when you move the pot, so be careful with it. The temperature control is part of the detachable cord.

Temperature & Recipe Times—Use the HIGH setting when recipes in this book say LOW. HIGH on this book is between HI and BROWN, with OFF at an 8 o'clock position. These pots reach selected temperature fast—usually in about 5 minutes. This is so much quicker than crockery-lined pots that the cooking times for recipes in this book must be reduced. On an 8 to 10 hour recipe, reduce cooking time to 6 to 8 hours. For shorter times, reduce the total time by 1/4 to 1/2.

Cleaning—These cookers are immersible and easily cleaned. Follow the Use and Care chapter recommendations for cleaning Teflon.

Regal Mardi Gras Pot O' Plenty

Usable capacity 4 quarts. This combination cooker/fryer uses Teflon II on the cooking surface. The outside finish is a scratch-resistant material called Lexan. The lid is metal. The plastic outer case insulates the pot and you can safely handle it after a day's cooking. Heating elements are on the bottom. This is not a "set it and forget it" pot—you must watch your food while using it—at least until you have learned how to use the temperature settings and cooking times. Hot spots at the bottom of the pot can burn your food so you should plan to turn meats and stir occasionally to avoid scorching.

Temperature & Recipe Times—The temperature control lever is continuously variable with indications 1 to 8. There is considerable "play" in the lever and any setting you choose is only an approximation. To use recipes in this book set at 2 for LOW and 3 for HIGH. This pot heats quicker than crockery-lined pots and cooking times must be reduced accordingly. For 8 to 10 hour recipes try cooking times of 6 to 8 hours. For shorter recipe times, reduce the total time by 1/4 to 1/2.

Cleaning—Do not immerse this pot. Fill it with warm water to soak off stubborn food. Teflon II makes the pot easy to clean. The Use and Care chapter tells how to clean Teflon II.

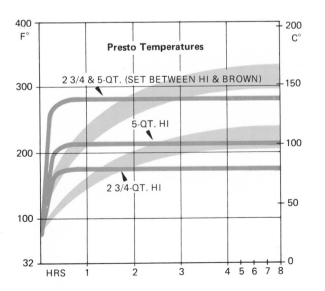

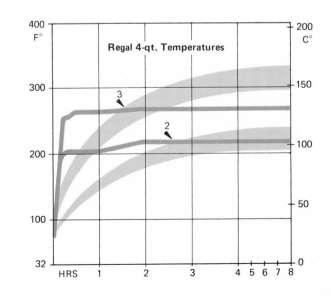

Regal Poly Pot

Usable capacity 5 quarts. This large cooker has white Teflon II on the aluminum cooking surface. A glass lid covers the wide-mouthed pot. The scratch-resistant Lexan outer case insulates the pot and you can safely handle the case after a day's cooking. A short cord is attached.

Temperature & Recipe Times—There is no manual temperature setting on this pot. The pot is ON when plugged in. To turn it OFF, unplug the cord. An automatic heat control cooks between the recipe HIGH and LOW temperatures. Recipes indicating HI must be cooked 2-4 hours more than the longest recipe time given. A 6-8 hour recipe needs to be cooked 10-12 hours. Recipes indicating LOW must be cooked about 2 hours less than the times given. A 6-8 hour recipe needs to be cooked 4-6 hours.

Cleaning—Do not immerse pot. Fill it with warm soapy water to soak off stubborn food. Teflon II makes the pot easy to clean. Use and Care chapter tells how to clean Teflon II.

Reliable 5 1/2-quart Crockery Slow Cooker

Usable capacity 5 quarts. This extra-large pot is designed for large recipes. The deep crockery liner has a painted-metal case with an attached cord. Wraparound heating elements in this pot are designed for cooking large quantities and the inside and outside of the pot become very hot. Use hot pads and *caution* in handling the pot and glass lid.

Temperature and Recipe Times—Our tests showed much higher temperatures than for other brands because this pot is designed for large quantity recipes. To use this pot with our recipe times and temperature settings, double 4-6 serving recipe quantities or reduce cooking times. Recipes indicating LOW must be reduced about an hour for a 6-hour recipe. Recipes that cook 4-8 hours on HIGH must be reduced 1/4 or more of the indicated time to avoid overcooking.

Cleaning—This pot is not immersible. Fill the empty pot with warm soapy water to soak off stubborn food. Follow the Use and Care chapter recommendations for cleaning crockery. Use warm soapy water and a damp cloth to wipe off the sides.

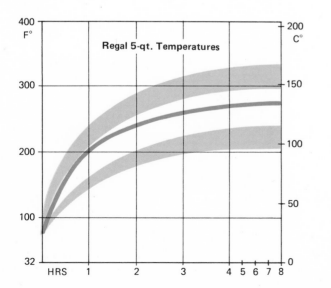

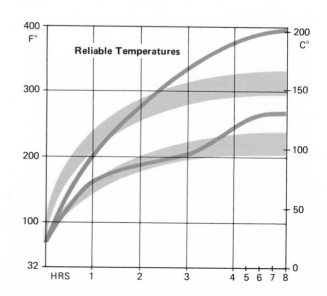

3 1/2 quart

4 1/2 & 5 quart

Rival Crock-Pots

All models have crockery liners with clear glass or Lexan plastic lids. Wraparound heating elements provide even heating from top to bottom. Cords are attached on some models, detachable with the temperature control on others. Accessories include a metal rack and baking pans with lids. The painted metal outside surface and glass lid of all models except the 3, 4 1/2, and 5-qt. models get very hot and you should use hot pads and caution in handling the pot and lid. The Lexan surface of the 3, 4 1/2, and 5-qt. models remains reasonably cool, even when the pot has been on all day.

Temperature & Recipe Times—Temperature settings of LOW and HIGH are exactly as found in the recipes. Cooking times are the same as provided in the recipes. Detachable temperature control units must be pushed all the way into the pot. Turn the knob *exactly* to LOW or HIGH or the pot will not heat.

Cleaning—These pots are not immersible. Fill the empty pot with warm water to soak off stubborn food. Follow the Use and Care chapter recommendations for cleaning crockery.

2-quart Stoneware Cooker—Usable capacity 1 3/4 quarts. This pot is good for one or two people. Ingredients for 4 to 5 serving recipes must be cut in half to fit this pot.

3-quart Casserole Cooker/Server—Usable capacity 2 1/2 quarts. Has removable crockery bowl (10-inch diameter) which is oven proof and dishwasher safe. When you use the bowl in the refrigerator, allow it to warm up to room temperature before re-heating. You can put the bowl in warm—not hot—water to hasten warming. Do not turn pot ON before inserting bowl or you may break the crock. Four to five serving recipes fit this pot.

3 1/2-quart Electric Slow Cooker—Usable capacity 3 quarts. Use 4 to 5 serving recipes with this popular model.

3 1/2-quart Deluxe Buffet Cooker—Usable capacity 3 quarts. Use 4 to 5 serving recipes with this pot. The feet and handles and a detachable cord are features which are different from the standard model.

4 1/2- and 5-quart Deluxe Cooker/Server—Usable capacity 4 quarts. Both models are exactly the same. The 10-inch-diameter pot will hold most roasts, chickens and large meals. Some 4 to 5 serving recipes can be doubled for use in this pot. Cooking times stay the same.

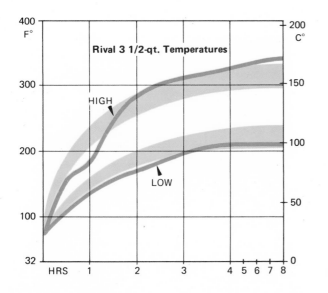

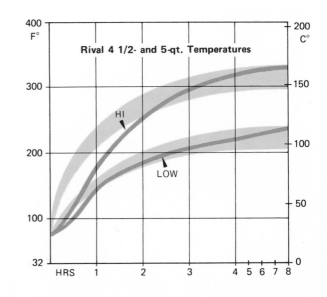

4-quart integrated model

Sears 4-quart Crockery Cooker (also Simpsons)

Usable capacity 3 1/2 quarts. This crockery pot has a glass lid, painted metal outside finish and attached cord.

The sides and lid get very hot so use a pot holder to remove the lid. Pick up the pot only by the handles.

Temperature & Recipe Times—Heating from the sides provides even heat distribution from top to bottom. This pot fits recipe temperatures and cooking times exactly. The temperature switch has two positions, MED and HI. For recipes in this book MED equals LOW and HI equals HIGH.

Cleaning—Do not immerse to clean. Fill empty pot with water to soak off stubborn food. Use and Care chapter tells how to clean crockery.

Sears Tray Model Crockery Cookers (also Simpsons)

These cookers have an electric heating base and a separate crockery pot with glass lid. The painted rectangular heating base has wooden handles and an attached cord. The pot sits in a shallow well in the heating base.

The crockery pots are dishwasher and oven safe, but you should not place the pot on any stove burner because that could break the pot. Always put ingredients into the pot *before* placing it on the heating base. Turn on the heat only after the crockery pot with contents has been placed in the heating well.

WARNING: At least one cup of liquid must be part of any recipe used in these pots. Do not let the pot operate dry for

5-quart tray model

baking and do not let all of the liquid evaporate or the pot will overheat and probably break.

The heating base may be used to warm food in pots or pans, but don't use the heating surface for a griddle. Both the pot and base get very hot, so use hot pads or mitts to handle either one. Do not attempt to move the base without pot holders, even though there are wooden handles. These wooden ends offer little protection against burning your hands. The heating bases smoke at first as the heating element warms up and burns off protective coatings.

Temperature & Recipe Times—For recipes in this book, set the 5-quart temperature controls to 2 for LOW and 3 for HIGH. Position 1 is too cool to cook food because it is designed for warming. Use the times given in the recipes. See special temperature note with 2 1/2-quart pot described below.

Cleaning—Never immerse the heating base in water. Wipe it clean with a damp cloth when it is completely cool. The Use and Care chapter tells how to clean crockery.

2 1/2-quart—Usable capacity 2 quarts. This pot is ideal for one or two people. To use the 4 to 6 serving recipes in this book, reduce the ingredients by 1/2. Setting 3 on the control is equal to LOW in the recipes. Because this pot will not attain high temperatures equal to the HIGH settings recommended in some recipes, use only those recipes which cook on LOW for the entire period.

5-quart—Usable capacity 4 1/2 quarts.

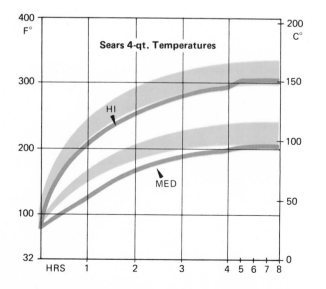

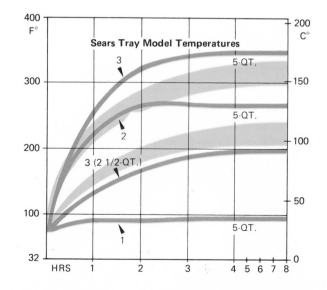

Sunbeam Crocker Cooker Fryer

Usable capacity 4 quarts. This unit cooks slowly and has a removable crockery pot. The heavy-wall pot provides even heat distribution, even though heating is only from the bottom. A large lip on the pot makes it easy to handle. It is dishwasher safe and oven proof. This unit is both a cooker and a fryer with a Teflon-coated cooking surface. It can be used for deep frying.

Temperature & Recipe Times—For recipes in this book use 200°F. for LOW. There is no 200°F. marker on the dial, so set it just left of the red CROCKERY band. For HIGH, set it between 325°F. and 350°F. Cooking times in the recipes are exactly right for this pot.

Cleaning—To clean, remove the empty pot and fill with warm water to soak off stubborn food. The slow cooker/fryer heating portion does not get very dirty with slow cooking. Wiping with a damp cloth will usually clean off any spilled food. Do not immerse the cooker/fryer unit.

Sunbeam Crocker Frypan

Usable capacity 2 quarts. This Teflon-coated electric frypan has a removable crockery insert. The fryer and insert are square-shaped and the lid is domed so the pot can hold pieces of meat or poultry somewhat taller than the depth of the pot. This model does not cook like other crockery-lined slow-cooking pots because the shallow crock liner exposes a lot of the food surface. Heating this shallow crock from the bottom heats the food unevenly and tends to cause the food to dry out. This causes faster cooking and requires frequent stirring to prevent sticking. Meats must be turned to ensure even doneness. Some recipes, especially soups and beans, can be used successfully in this pot.

Temperature & Recipe Times—For recipes in this book, use 200°F. for LOW and 300°F. for HIGH. Cooking times in the recipes may be shortened 1/4 to 1/2 for use with this pot. If you are cooking something which does not stick up into the lid area, add a piece of aluminum foil over the food to help get the temperatures more even throughout the pot. This will also speed the cooking.

Cleaning—Remove the empty crock and fill with warm water to soak off stubborn food. The frypan heating portion does not get very dirty with slow cooking. Wiping with a damp cloth will usually clean off any spilled food. Do not immerse the frypan unit. The Use and Care chapter details cleaning hints for crockery and Teflon.

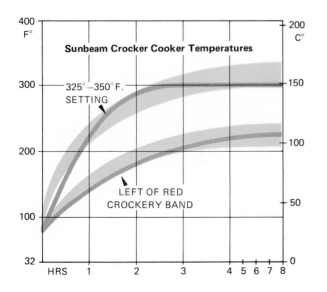

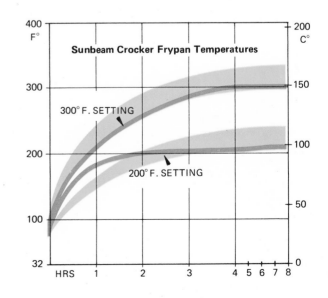

Van Wyck Sim·R·Pot
Robeson Sim·R·Pot
K-Mart LaCuisine Sim·R·Pot

Usable capacity 3 quarts. This popular pot fits most 4-5 serving recipes well. The pot has a painted metal outside surface with a white-glass liner and a clear-glass lid. The cord is attached. Do not touch the outside metal surface because it gets very hot. Plastic handles remain cool enough to handle, but it is best to use hot pads whenever you move or lift the pot or lid. Heating elements are wrapped around the pot.

Temperature & Recipe Times—Make sure to turn the control switch exactly to Sim·R·LO or Sim·R·HI. For recipes that cook on LOW, use times given in our recipes. Recipes which cook on HIGH will require at least an additional 2 hours and perhaps more.

Cleaning—Because this pot is not immersible, fill it with warm soapy water to soak off stubborn food. Wipe off the outside with a damp cloth. The Use and Care chapter explains how to clean glass liners.

Van Wyck Sim·R·Ware (also Wards and others)

Usable capacity 4 quarts. These glass-lined pots have glass lids. Wraparound heating element provides even heating from top to bottom. The cord is detachable. The outside of the pot and lid get very hot. Use a pot holder or mitts to remove the lid and pick up the pot only with the handles. This pot was supplied in 11 different trims for different stores and chain stores. It was discontinued in 1975.

Temperature & Recipe Times—As you can see in the temperature chart, this pot does not get very hot. Use the HIGH setting whenever the recipe calls for LOW. Recipes requiring HIGH settings will have to be cooked several extra hours to be done.

Cleaning—Do not immerse this unit in water. Fill empty cooker with warm soapy water to wash it. See Use and Care chapter for hints on cleaning the glass liner without using abrasives.

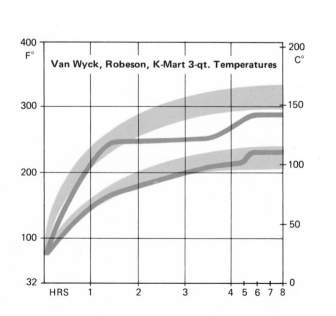

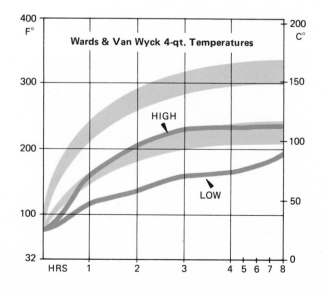

Wards 5 1/2-quart Crockery Slow Cooker

Usable capacity 5 quarts. This extra-large pot is designed for large recipes. The deep crockery liner has a painted-metal case with an attached cord. Wraparound heating elements in this pot are designed for cooking large quantities and the inside and outside of the pot become very hot. Use hot pads and *caution* in handling the pot and glass lid.

Temperature and Recipe Times—Our tests showed much higher temperatures than for other brands because this pot is designed for large quantity recipes. To use this pot with our recipe times and temperature settings, double 4-6 serving recipe quantities or reduce cooking times. Recipes indicating LOW must be reduced about an hour for a 6-hour recipe. Recipes that cook 4-8 hours on HIGH must be reduced 1/4 or more of the indicated time to avoid overcooking.

Cleaning—This pot is not immersible. Fill the empty pot with warm soapy water to soak off stubborn food. Follow the Use and Care chapter recommendations for cleaning crockery. Use warm soapy water and a damp cloth to wipe off the sides.

Wear · Ever Pokey · Pot

Usable capacity 3 quarts. This pot is available with either a removable brown ceramic crock or a white-glass liner. The units cook exactly alike. The removable container sets in a separate heating pot containing fully insulated heating elements. The heating pot is aluminum with a porcelain finish. The temperature control detaches with its cord. The lid is glass. The liners are dishwasher and oven-safe, but you should not place them on a stove burner or electric element because this will break the crockery or glass. Do not turn the heating pot on before inserting the crock or glass liner.

Temperature & Recipe Times—This pot fits our recipe temperatures and times for LOW. Shorten recipe times on HIGH by 2 hours or more.

Cleaning—Do not immerse the heating pot in water. Wipe it clean with a damp cloth when it is completely cool. The Use and Care chapter tells how to clean crockery and glass liners.

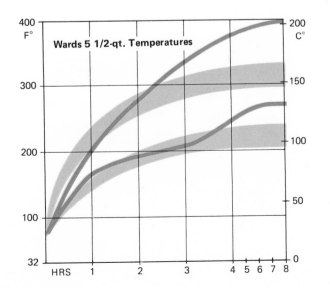

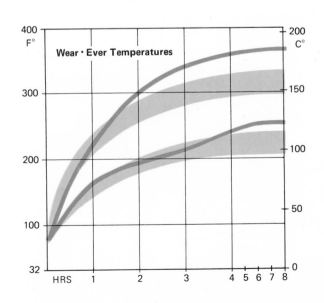

West Bend Colonial Crock® (foreground) and Beans 'N Stuff® Slo-Cookers

Usable capacity 2 quarts. Stoneware pot and lid, separate low-wattage heating base. Don't heat base before setting pot on it or pot may break. Pot can be used in your oven at temperatures to 425°F *if you preheat the oven first.* Do not use pot on gas or electric range as direct heat could crack the pot. Heating base works as a warming/cooking unit for other pans or coffee pots, but do not use as a griddle. Do not carry or move heating base when it is hot. Use hot pads to handle the pot and lid.

Temperature & Recipe Times —Colonial Crock settings: L, 1, 2, 3, 4 and H. Unplug cord to turn OFF. Set to 4 or H and use recipes which cook on LOW. Beans 'N Stuff does not have variable control. Use recipes which cook on LOW. Heating base will not attain temperatures suitable for HIGH in recipes.

Cleaning —Follow Use and Care chapter directions for crockery. Do not soak pot or lid for long periods because nonglazed pot and lid bottom surfaces will absorb water. Before storing, let pot and lid stand inverted until completely dry. When washed in a dishwasher, the normal drying cycle will dry out the stoneware. Do not immerse heating base in water. When cool, wipe clean with a damp cloth.

West Bend 4 Qt. Slo-Cooker

Usable capacity 3 1/2 quarts. This porcelain coated aluminum pot has a No-Stick coated cooking surface. The lid is glass. The pot can be used in the oven at preheated temperatures up to 350°F. You can also use the pot on gas or electric ranges, provided flames or heat do not come up the sides to damage the handles.

The heating base may be used as a warming and cooking unit for other pans or non-electric coffeemakers, but do not use the heating surface as a griddle. Do not try to carry or move the base while it is hot. Carry the pot or handle the lid only with hot pads.

Temperature & Recipe Times —The temperature control has settings from 1 to 5. Dial can also be set in between settings. There is no setting for OFF; unplug the cord to turn OFF. Use the 2-1/2 setting and the same times for recipes which cook on LOW. Recipes calling for a HIGH setting should be cooked on the 4 setting.

Cleaning —Follow Use and Care chapter directions for porcelain and No-Stick finishes. The pot is immersible and can be cleaned in the sink or dishwasher. If you use a dishwasher, recondition the cooking surface with cooking oil before reusing the pot. Do not immerse heating base in water. Wipe it clean with a damp cloth when it is cool.

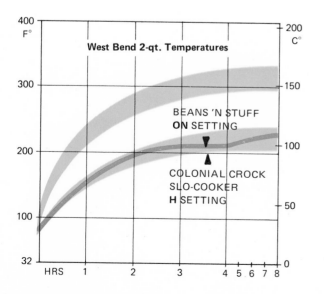

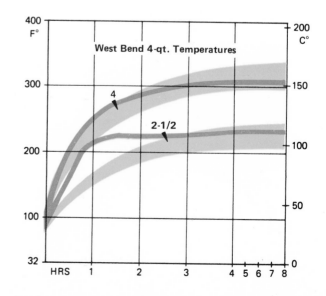

West Bend Lazy Day® Slo-Cooker

Usable capacity 5 quarts. This porcelain-coated steel pot and lid are used with separate heating base. You can also use the pot on gas or electric ranges, provided flames or heat do not come up the side of the pot to damage the handles.

The heating base may be used as a warming and cooking unit for other pans or non-electric coffee makers, but do not use the heating surface as a griddle. Do not try to carry or move the heating base when it is hot. Carry the pot only by the handles.

Temperature & Recipe Times—The temperature control has settings from 1 to 5. Dial can also be set in between settings. There is no setting for OFF; unplug the cord to turn OFF. For recipes in this book, set dial at 2-1/2 for LOW and 4 for HIGH. Recipe times are the same as those in the recipes.

Cleaning—Follow Use and Care chapter directions for porcelain and No-Stick finishes. The pot can be cleaned in the sink or dishwasher as it is immersible. Do not immerse heating base in water. Wipe it clean with a damp cloth when it is cool.

West Bend Slo-Cooker Plus™ Automatic Cooker

Usable capacity 5 quarts. Porcelain on aluminum pot has a No-Stick coated cooking surface. Pot is separate from the heating base and can be used without the base in the oven at preheated temperatures up to 350°F. Pot can also be used for top-of-the-range cooking. Pot has a glass cover. Baking or roasting rack also included.

The heating base has a No-Stick coated surface and can be used as a mini-griddle. Do not carry or move the heating base when it is hot. Carry the pot only by the handles.

Temperature & Recipe Times—The temperature control has settings from 1 to 5. Dial can also be set in between settings. There is no OFF position; unplug cord to turn OFF. For recipes in this book, set dial at 3 for LOW and 5 for HIGH. Recipe times are the same as those in the recipes.

Cleaning—Follow Use and Care chapter directions for No-Stick finishes. The pot can be cleaned in the sink or dishwasher as it is immersible. After dishwasher cleaning, pot should be reconditioned with cooking oil. Do not immerse heating base in water. When base is cool, wipe it with a damp cloth.

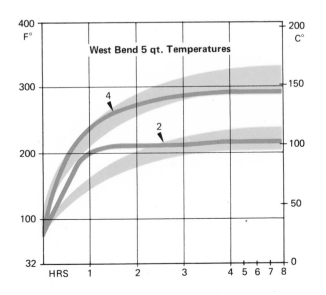

West Bend 5 qt. Temperatures

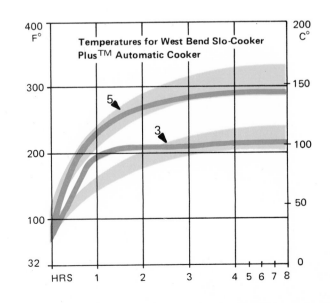

Temperatures for West Bend Slo-Cooker Plus™ Automatic Cooker

BEEF

Slow-cooked beef is fabulous! You can stretch your penny-pincher budget by buying cheaper, less tender cuts. The pot makes them super tender—and you end up with more flavor and vitamins. Surprise! You get less shrinkage than with other cooking methods.

Here are some secrets for slow cooking beef successfully. The first: Some vegetables take as long or longer to cook than beef. If you plan a beef dish with large chunks of carrots or celery, place these in the bottom or around the sides of the pot. And, cover them with liquid such as water, bouillon or tomato sauce. You may want to cut them slightly smaller than usual. Slow cookers are notoriously slow when cooking vegetables and smaller pieces cook faster.

Another secret: The good juices of the meat don't evaporate. As a result, you get more liquid with that rich, meaty flavor—a special treat for sauce and gravy lovers. In most cases you can stir in cornstarch or dissolved flour after the meat is done. Then cook on HIGH for a few minutes to thicken the gravy.

It is not necessary to brown meat before you cook. But, if the meat is fatty, browning first and pouring off the excess fat is usually helpful. Ordinarily, you can place most beef cuts directly in the bottom of the pot with the seasonings and vegetables. But, if the meat is really fatty or you don't want it to cook in the juices, put it on a rack in the bottom of the pot.

You will notice a wide range of cooking times for all of the beef recipes. That's another advantage of slow cookers—you can take off in the morning, leave the meat cooking most of the day and not worry about it sticking, burning or overcooking should you return later than expected. The low temperature is so low that an hour or two makes very little difference in slow-cooking recipes.

How do you decide when the beef is done? Cook until the minimum time suggested for the recipe. Then, just remove the meat from the slow-cooking pot and stick it with a fork to see if it is as tender as your family prefers. The thickness of the cut of beef, distribution of fat and amount of bone will change the cooking time, so always check before assuming the meat is ready to serve.

CREOLE STEAK STRIPS

1 1/2 lbs. boneless round steak
Salt and pepper
1 onion, chopped
1 cup sliced celery
1 cup seasoned tomato juice
2 tsp. Worcestershire sauce

1/8 tsp. garlic powder
1 medium green pepper, chopped
1 (10-oz.) package frozen or 1 1/2 cups fresh okra
1 (2 1/2-oz.) can sliced mushrooms, drained
Carrots curls (optional)

Cut steak into strips about 1/2 inch wide and 2 inches long. Sprinkle with salt and pepper. Place in slow-cooking pot with onion, celery, tomato juice, Worcestershire sauce, and garlic powder. Cover and cook on low 6 to 8 hours. Turn control to high. Add green peppers and partially thawed okra and mushrooms. Cover and cook on high for 30 minutes or until okra is done. Garnish with carrot curls if desired. Serve over rice. Makes 5 to 6 servings.

MEXICAN BEEF

1 1/2 to 2 lbs. boneless round steak
1 clove garlic, minced
1/4 tsp. pepper
1/2 tsp. salt
1 tbs. chili powder

1 tbs. prepared mustard
1 onion, chopped
1 beef bouillon cube, crushed
1 (16-oz.) can tomatoes, cut up
1 (16-oz.) can kidney beans, drained

Spread meat with mixture of garlic, pepper, salt, chili powder, and mustard. Cut into 1/2-inch wide strips. Place in slow-cooking pot. Cover with onion, bouillon cube, and tomatoes. Cover and cook on low for 6 to 8 hours. Turn control to high. Add beans and cook, covered, for 30 minutes. Serve on bed of rice. Makes 5 to 6 servings.

Courtesy National Livestock & Meat Board

Creole Steak Strips   Courtesy National Livestock & Meat Board

Round Steak With Rich Gravy   Courtesy National Livestock & Meat Board

ROUND STEAK WITH RICH GRAVY

2 to 2 1/2 lbs. round steak
1 (1 1/2-oz.) package onion soup mix

1/4 cup water
1 (10 1/2-oz.) can condensed cream of mushroom soup

Cut steak into 5 or 6 serving-size pieces. Place in slow-cooking pot. Add dry onion soup mix, water, and condensed mushroom soup. Cover and cook on low for 6 to 8 hours. Excellent when served with mashed potatoes. Makes 5 or 6 servings.

ROUND STEAK ITALIANO

1 1/2 lbs. round steak
1 tsp. salt
1/2 tsp. oregano

1/4 tsp. pepper
1 (15 1/2-oz.) jar spaghetti sauce with mushrooms
1 (16-oz.) can whole small onions, drained

Cut steak into 5 or 6 serving-size pieces. Coat with salt, oregano, and pepper. In slow-cooking pot, pour spaghetti sauce over meat. Cover and cook on low for 7 to 9 hours or until meat is tender. Turn control to high; add onions. Cook on high for 10 to 15 minutes. Serve with Italian green beans and toasted garlic cheese bread. Makes 5 to 6 servings.

Budget Beef Stroganoff   Courtesy California Beef Council

BUDGET BEEF STROGANOFF

1 1/2 to 2 lbs. round steak
1 tsp. salt
1/8 tsp. pepper
1 onion, sliced
1/4 tsp. garlic salt
1 tbs. Worcestershire sauce

1 1/2 cups beef bouillon
1 tbs. catsup
2 tbs. dry white wine
1/4 lb. fresh mushrooms, sliced
1/3 cup flour
1 cup dairy sour cream

Cut steak into 1/4-inch strips. Coat with salt and pepper. Drop into bottom of slow-cooking pot with onion. Mix garlic salt, Worcestershire sauce, bouillon, and catsup. Pour over meat. Cover and cook on low for 6 to 8 hours or until tender. Turn control to high. Add wine and mushrooms. Dissolve flour in small amount of water. Add to meat mixture, stirring until blended. Cook on high for 15 minutes or until slightly thickened. Stir in sour cream; turn off heat. Serve with rice or noodles. Makes 5 to 6 servings.

SWEDISH STYLE STEAK

2 to 2 1/2 lbs. boneless round steak
Salt and pepper
1 tsp. dill weed
1 medium onion, sliced
1 bouillon cube, crumbled

1/2 cup water
1/4 cup flour
1/4 cup water
1 cup dairy sour cream

Cut steak into serving-size pieces. Sprinkle with salt and pepper. Place in slow-cooking pot. Add dill, onion, bouillon cube and 1/2 cup water. Cover and cook on low for 6 to 8 hours. Remove meat. Thicken juices with flour dissolved in 1/4 cup cold water. Turn control to high; cook 10 minutes or until slightly thickened. Stir in sour cream. Turn off heat. Serve sauce over meat, with mashed potatoes or noodles. Makes 6 to 8 servings.

SWISS BEEF BIRDS

2 lbs. round steak, 1/2 inch thick
2 medium carrots
1 large dill pickle
2 tbs. flour
1 tsp. salt
1/4 tsp. pepper

1/8 tsp. garlic salt
2 tbs. salad oil
1 (8-oz.) can tomato sauce
1 small onion, chopped
2 tbs. minced parsley

With meat mallet, pound steak until 1/4 inch thick; cut into 5 or 6 serving pieces. Cut each carrot into thin sticks and the pickle into 5 or 6 strips. Place several carrot sticks and one pickle stick on each piece of meat. Beginning at narrow end, roll up, securing with small skewers or toothpicks. Mix flour with salt, pepper, and garlic salt; coat rolls, reserving remaining mixture. In large skillet or slow-cooking pot with browning unit, brown meat rolls in hot oil. Pour off excess fat. Place browned meat in slow-cooking pot. Mix tomato sauce with reserved flour; stir in onion. Pour over meat. Cover and simmer on low for 7 to 9 hours or until tender. Sprinkle with parsley. Makes 5 or 6 servings.

SWISS STEAK

1 1/2 to 2 lbs. round steak
2 tbs. flour
1 tsp. salt
1/8 tsp. pepper
2 tbs. salad oil

1 (16-oz.) can tomatoes, cut up
1 large onion, sliced
1 stalk celery, thinly sliced
1 tbs. thick bottled steak sauce

Cut steak into serving-size pieces. Coat with flour, salt, and pepper. In large skillet or slow-cooking pot with browning unit, brown meat in oil. Pour off excess fat. In slow-cooking pot, combine meat with tomatoes, onion, celery, and steak sauce. Cover pot and cook on low for 6 to 8 hours or until tender. Thicken juices with additional flour dissolved in a small amount of water, if desired. Makes 5 to 6 servings.

CHINESE PEPPER STEAK

1 to 1 1/2 lbs. round steak
2 tbs. oil
1 clove garlic, minced
1 /2 tsp. salt
1/4 tsp. pepper
1/4 cup soy sauce
1 tsp. sugar

1 cup fresh or canned bean sprouts, drained
1 cup canned tomatoes, cut up
2 green peppers, seeded and cut into strips
1 tbs. cornstarch
2 tbs. cold water
4 green onions, sliced

Slice steak into narrow strips. In skillet or slow-cooking pot with browning unit, brown steak in oil. Combine with garlic, salt, pepper, soy sauce, and sugar in slow-cooking pot. Cook on low 6 to 8 hours. Turn control to high. Add bean sprouts, tomatoes, and green peppers. Dissolve cornstarch in water. Stir into pot. Cover and cook on high 15-20 minutes or until thickened. Sprinkle with onions. Makes 4 to 5 servings.

FLEMISH CARBONADES

2 to 3 lbs. boneless chuck, cut into 1-inch
    cubes
1/2 cup flour
1/4 cup butter or margarine
1 onion, sliced

1 tsp. salt
1/8 tsp. pepper
1 clove garlic, minced
2 cups beer
1/4 cup flour

Coat beef with 1/2 cup flour. In large skillet or slow-cooking pot with browning unit, brown meat in melted butter. Drain off excess fat. In slow-cooking pot, combine meat with onion, salt, pepper, garlic, and beer. Cover and cook on low for 5 to 7 hours or until meat is tender. Turn control to high. Dissolve remaining 1/4 cup flour in small amount of water. Stir into meat mixture; cook on high for 20 to 30 minutes. Makes 5 to 7 servings.

NEW ENGLAND CHUCK ROAST

1 (3-lb.) beef chuck roast
1 tsp. monosodium glutamate
1 tsp. salt
1/4 tsp. pepper
2 onions, cut into quarters
4 carrots, cut into quarters

1 stalk celery, cut into eight chunks
1 bay leaf
2 tbs. vinegar
5 cups water
1 small cabbage cut into wedges

Sauce:
3 tbs. butter or margarine
1 tbs. instant minced onion
2 tbs. flour

1 1/2 cups reserved beef broth
2 tbs. prepared horseradish
1/2 tsp. salt

Sprinkle meat with seasonings. Place onions, carrots, and celery in slow-cooking pot. Top with meat. Add bay leaf, vinegar and water. Cover pot and cook on low for 5 to 7 hours or until meat is tender. Remove meat; turn to high. Add cabbage wedges; cover and cook on high for 15 to 20 minutes or until cabbage is done. Meanwhile melt butter in saucepan. Stir in instant onion and flour. Drain 1 1/2 cups broth out of slow-cooking pot. Pour broth, horseradish and salt into saucepan. Cook over low heat, stirring constantly, until thickened and smooth. Serve sauce with roast and vegetables. Makes 6 servings.

New England Chuck Roast   Courtesy Ac'cent International

Chinese Beef and Pea Pods   Courtesy California Beef Council

CHINESE BEEF AND PEA PODS

1 (1 to 1 1/2 lb.) flank steak
1 (10 1/2-oz.) can condensed beef consomme
1/4 cup soy sauce
1/4 tsp. ground ginger
1 bunch green onions, sliced

2 tbs. cornstarch
2 tbs. cold water
1 (7-oz.) package frozen Chinese pea pods,
  partially thawed

Thinly slice flank steak diagonally across the grain. Combine strips in slow-cooking pot with consomme, soy sauce, ginger and onions. Cover and cook on low for 5 to 7 hours. Turn control to high. Stir in cornstarch that has been dissolved in the cold water. Cook on high for 10 to 15 minutes or until thickened. Drop in pea pods the last 5 minutes. Serve over hot rice. Makes 4 to 5 servings.

TERIYAKI STEAK

2 to 2 1/2 lbs. boneless chuck steak
1 tsp. ground ginger
1 tbs. sugar

2 tbs. oil
1/2 cup soy sauce
1 clove garlic, crushed

Cut steak into 1/8-inch thick slices. Combine remaining ingredients in small bowl. Place meat in slow-cooking pot. Pour sauce over. Cover and cook on low for 6 to 8 hours. Serve with rice. Makes 5 to 6 servings.

FLANK STEAK IN MUSHROOM SAUCE

1 (1 to 1 1/2 lb.) flank steak
1/4 cup sauterne wine
1 tbs. soy sauce
1 clove garlic, minced
1 (10 1/2-oz.) can beef broth
1 tbs. catsup

1 tsp. prepared mustard
1 tbs. instant minced onion
2 tbs. cornstarch
2 tbs. water
1/4 lb. fresh mushrooms, sliced

Place steak in slow-cooking pot. Combine sauterne, soy sauce, garlic, broth, catsup, mustard, and onion; pour over steak. Cover and cook on low for 6 to 8 hours. Dissolve cornstarch in water; stir into pot. Add mushrooms. Turn control to high; cover and cook on high 20 to 30 minutes or until mushrooms are done. Makes 4 to 5 servings.

FLANK STEAK CREOLE

1 1/2 to 2 lbs. flank steak
Salt and pepper
2 tbs. chopped green pepper
2 tbs. chopped onion
1 tbs. tomato paste
1/2 tsp. prepared horseradish

1/4 tsp. sugar
1/2 cup water
2 cups herb-seasoned stuffing mix
2 tbs. cornstarch
1/4 cup cold water
1 tbs. tomato paste

Score one side of meat. Sprinkle with salt and pepper. Combine green pepper, onion, 1 tbs. tomato paste, horseradish, sugar, 1/2 cup water, and stuffing. Spoon stuffing mixture down middle of unscored side of flank steak. Fold ends over and overlap long sides; skewer together. Place on metal rack or trivet in slow-cooking pot. Cover and cook on low for 8 to 10 hours. Remove meat. Turn control to high. Dissolve cornstarch in 1/4 cup cold water; stir in 1 tbs. tomato paste. Add to juices in pot. Cook on high for 15 to 20 minutes or until slightly thickened. Slice steak across the grain. Pass sauce with the steak. Makes 4 to 5 servings.

STUFFED FLANK STEAK

1 1/2 cups packaged bread stuffing
1 (3-oz.) can sliced mushrooms with juice
2 tbs. melted butter or margarine

2 tbs. grated Parmesan cheese
1 (1 to 1 1/2-lb.) flank steak, scored on both sides
2 tbs. salad oil

Sauce:
1 (3/4-oz.) package brown gravy mix
1/4 cup dry red wine

2 tbs. minced green onions
1/4 cup currant jelly

Combine bread stuffing with mushrooms and juice, butter, and cheese. Spread over flank steak; roll up like jelly roll. Fasten with skewers or string. Pour oil in slow-cooking pot. Roll steak in oil, coating all sides. *For Sauce:* Prepare gravy mix according to package directions. Pour gravy, wine, and onions over meat. Cover and cook on low 8 to 10 hours. Remove meat from pot; slice. Add jelly to sauce and stir until dissolved. Serve over meat. Makes 4 to 5 servings.

1/Score flank steak to make it flexible to roll.

2/Spread stuffing over flank steak. Roll up like jelly roll and fasten with skewers or string.

3/Pour sauce over meat.

Fruited Flank Steak Courtesy Cling Peach Advisory Board

FRUITED FLANK STEAK

1 (1 to 1 1/2-lb.) flank steak
Salt and pepper
1 (30-oz.) can fruit cocktail
1 tbs. salad oil

1 tbs. lemon juice
1/4 cup bottled teriyaki sauce
1 tsp. vinegar
1 clove garlic, minced

Sprinkle flank steak with salt and pepper; place in slow-cooking pot. Drain fruit cocktail, saving 1/4 cup syrup. Combine 1/4 cup syrup with remaining ingredients; pour over steak in pot. Cover and cook on low for 7 to 9 hours or until tender. Add drained fruit the last few minutes. Lift out of pot; place on platter. With sharp knife, cut thin slices of meat across the grain. Serve hot. Makes 4 to 5 servings.

BEEF BURGUNDY

2 slices bacon, chopped
2 lbs. sirloin tip or round steak, cut into
   1-inch cubes
1/4 cup flour
1 tsp. salt
1/2 tsp. seasoned salt
1/4 tsp. marjoram

1/4 tsp. thyme
1/4 tsp. pepper
1 clove garlic, minced
1 beef bouillon cube, crushed
1 cup Burgundy wine
1/4 lb. fresh mushrooms, sliced
2 tbs. cornstarch (optional)

In large skillet or slow-cooking pot with browning unit, cook bacon several minutes. Remove bacon and set aside. Coat beef with flour and brown on all sides in bacon mixture. Combine steak, bacon drippings, cooked bacon, seasonings, bouillon, and Burgundy in slow-cooking pot. Cover and cook on low for 6 to 8 hours or until meat is tender. Turn control to high. Add mushrooms; cook on high 15 minutes. To thicken sauce, if desired, add cornstarch (dissolved in 2 tbs. cold water) with mushrooms. Makes 6 servings.

RANCH STYLE BEEF

2 lbs. boneless beef stew meat, cut into
   1 1/2-inch cubes
12 to 14 small white onions
4 whole cloves
2 tbs. brown sugar
1 1/2 tsp. salt

1/2 tsp. bottled brown gravy sauce
1 tbs. red wine vinegar
1 bay leaf
1/8 tsp. thyme
3/4 cup water
1/4 cup flour

In slow-cooking pot, alternate beef and onions; stick cloves into 4 onions. Sprinkle with sugar and salt. Combine gravy sauce, vinegar, bay leaf, thyme, and water. Pour over meat. Cover and cook on low for 5 to 7 hours or until tender. Turn control to high. Dissolve flour in small amount of water. Stir into meat juices. Cook on high for 15 to 20 minutes. Makes 6 servings.

FARM STYLE STEW

1 1/2 lbs. beef stew meat, cut into 1-inch
   cubes
1 tsp. salt
1/4 tsp. pepper
1/2 tsp. paprika
1/2 tsp. seasoned salt

4 medium zucchini, cut into 1-inch slices
2 cups hot water
2 tbs. bottled steak sauce
1 (17-oz.) can whole kernel corn, drained
3 tbs. cornstarch
3 tbs. cold water

Sprinkle beef with salt, pepper, paprika, and seasoned salt. Place in slow-cooking pot with zucchini; pour hot water and steak sauce over. Cover and cook on low for 7 to 9 hours or until tender. Turn control to high. Stir in corn. Dissolve cornstarch in cold water; add to meat mixture. Cook on high for 15 to 20 minutes. Makes 5 to 6 servings.

OLD FASHIONED BEEF STEW

2 lbs. beef stew meat, cut into 1 1/2-inch
  cubes
1/2 cup flour
2 tbs. oil
1 bay leaf
1 tbs. Worcestershire sauce
1 onion, chopped
1 cup beef bouillon
1/4 tsp. pepper

2 tsp. salt
1 tsp. sugar
6 carrots, peeled and sliced or quartered
1 cup sliced celery
4 potatoes, peeled and cut into eighths
12 small white onions
2 medium turnips, peeled and quartered (optional)
4 cups water
1 cup cooked okra (optional)

Coat meat with flour; set excess flour aside. In large skillet or slow-cooking pot with browning unit, heat oil. Brown meat on all sides. In slow-cooking pot, combine browned beef, bay leaf, Worcestershire sauce, chopped onion, bouillon, pepper, salt, sugar, and vegetables. Pour water over all. Cover and cook on low 8 to 10 hours. Turn control on high. Thicken with flour left over from coating (about 1/4 cup) dissolved in a small amount of water. Add okra if desired. Cover and cook on high 10 to 15 minutes or until slightly thickened. Makes 6 to 8 servings.

OXTAIL STEW

4 lbs. oxtails, cut into 2-inch lengths
1/4 cup flour
Salt and pepper
2 tbs. salad oil
1 medium tomato, peeled and chopped
1 onion, chopped
3 carrots, chopped

2 turnips, chopped
1 clove garlic, crushed
1 bay leaf
3 cups beef bouillon
1 cup port wine
1/2 tsp. pepper
2 leeks, sliced

Coat meat with flour; sprinkle with salt and pepper. In large skillet or slow-cooking pot with browning unit, brown meat in oil. Drain off excess fat. Combine browned meat in slow-cooking pot with remaining ingredients. Cover and cook on low for 7 to 9 hours. Remove bay leaf and oxtails. Cut meat off bones; dice and return to stew. Let stand a few minutes; skim excess fat off top.* Makes 6 to 8 servings.

*If time permits, refrigerate stew; skim off excess cold fat and then reheat stew at serving time.

BARBECUED BEEF & BEANS

2 to 2 1/2 lbs. beef stew meat, cut into 1-inch
  cubes
Salt and pepper

1 cup smoke-flavored barbecue sauce
1 cup beef bouillon
2 (1-lb.) cans dry lima beans, drained

Sprinkle beef with salt and pepper. Place in slow-cooking pot with barbecue sauce and bouillon. Cover and cook on low for 4 to 6 hours. Add drained beans and cook on high 15 to 20 minutes. Makes 6 servings.

Old Fashioned Beef Stew   Courtesy Florida Department of Citrus

SOUTHWESTERN BEEF & BEANS

1 lb. dried pinto beans
6 cups cold water
1/2 lb. salt pork, cut up
1 lb. lean chuck steak, cut into 1-inch cubes
1 red chili pepper or 1/2 tsp. crushed red
    pepper
1 medium onion, chopped

2 cloves garlic, minced
1 (6-oz.) can tomato paste
1 1/2 tbs. chili powder
1 tsp. salt
1 tsp. cumin seed
1/2 tsp. marjoram leaves

Soak beans in water overnight. Brown salt pork in skillet or slow-cooking pot with browning unit. In slow-cooking pot, combine soaked beans (with water), browned pork, and remaining ingredients. Cover and cook on low for 9 to 10 hours. Makes 8 servings.

SPANISH STYLE LIVER

2 lbs. sliced beef or calves liver
4 slices bacon, cut in half
1/2 cup chopped carrot
1/2 cup chopped celery
1 small onion, sliced

1 (1-lb.) can stewed tomatoes
1 tsp. salt
1/8 tsp. pepper
1 small bay leaf

Place liver in slow-cooking pot. Arrange bacon on top. Mix remaining ingredients and pour over liver. Cover and cook on low 6 to 8 hours. Remove bay leaf. Makes 5 to 6 servings.

MARCO POLO SHORT RIBS

4 lbs. beef short ribs
1 large tomato, chopped
1 cup beef bouillon
1/4 cup Burgundy wine
1 tbs. instant minced onion

2 tbs. prepared horseradish
1 tsp. salt
1/4 tsp. pepper
1/4 tsp. ground ginger
2 tbs. cornstarch

In large skillet or slow-cooking pot with browning unit, brown short ribs; drain off fat. In slow-cooking pot, combine meat with remaining ingredients except cornstarch. Cover and cook on low for 6 to 8 hours. Turn control to high. Remove meat from pot. Skim excess fat off top of meat broth. Dissolve cornstarch in small amount of cold water; stir into meat juices in pot. Cook on high for 15 to 20 minutes or until slightly thickened. Serve over meat. Makes 4 to 6 servings.

Southwestern Beef & Beans   Courtesy California Dry Bean Advisory Board

Spanish Style Liver   Courtesy National Livestock & Meat Board

Home-Style Short Ribs   Courtesy California Beef Council

HOME-STYLE SHORT RIBS

3 to 4 lbs. lean beef short ribs
4 potatoes, peeled and quartered
4 carrots, peeled and quartered
1 onion, sliced
2 tbs. vinegar
2 tsp. sugar
1 tbs. horseradish

1 tbs. prepared mustard
2 tbs. catsup
1 cup beef bouillon
1 tsp. salt
1/4 tsp. pepper
1/4 cup flour

In large skillet or slow-cooking pot with browning unit, brown short ribs; drain off excess fat. Place potatoes, carrots and onion in slow-cooking pot. Arrange browned ribs over vegetables. Combine vinegar, sugar, horseradish, mustard, catsup, bouillon, salt and pepper. Pour over meat. Cover and cook on low for 6 to 8 hours or until meat is tender. Remove short ribs and vegetables. Turn control to high. Dissolve flour in small amount of water. Stir into sauce; cook on high for 10 to 15 minutes or until thickened. Serve with meat and vegetables. Makes 4 to 6 servings.

MEXICAN STYLE SHORT RIBS

3 to 4 lbs. beef short ribs
1 (10 1/2-oz.) can beef consomme

1 (1 1/4-oz.) package taco seasoning mix
1/4 cup chopped green pepper

In large skillet or slow-cooking pot with browning unit, brown short ribs; pour off excess fat. Mix beef consomme with dry taco mix; add green pepper. In slow-cooking pot, pour sauce over ribs. Cover and cook on low for 6 to 8 hours. Makes 5 to 6 servings.

GERMAN SHORT RIBS

3 to 3 1/2 lbs. beef short ribs
2 tbs. flour
1 tsp. salt
1/8 tsp. pepper
2 tbs. shortening
2 medium onions, sliced
1/2 cup dry red wine

1/2 cup chili sauce*
3 tbs. brown sugar
3 tbs. vinegar
1 tbs. Worcestershire sauce
1/2 tsp. dry mustard
1/2 tsp. chili powder
2 tbs. flour

Coat short ribs in mixture of 2 tablespoons flour with salt and pepper. Melt shortening in large skillet or slow-cooking pot with browning unit; add ribs and brown on all sides. Pour off excess fat. In slow-cooking pot, combine ribs, onions, wine, chili sauce, brown sugar, vinegar, Worcestershire sauce, mustard, and chili powder. Cover and cook on low for 6 to 8 hours. Turn control to high. Thicken with 2 tbs. flour that has been dissolved in a small amount of water. Cook on high about 10 minutes or until slightly thickened. Serve over wide noodles. Makes 5 to 6 servings.

*Bottled tomato sauce similar to catsup.

HUNGARIAN GOULASH

2 lbs. beef stew meat, cut into 1-inch cubes
1 large onion, sliced
1 clove garlic, minced
1/2 cup catsup
2 tbs. Worcestershire sauce
1 tbs. brown sugar

2 tsp. salt
2 tsp. paprika
1/2 tsp. dry mustard
1 cup water
1/4 cup flour

Place meat in slow-cooking pot; cover with sliced onion. Combine garlic, catsup, Worcestershire sauce, sugar, salt, paprika, and mustard. Stir in water. Pour over meat. Cover and cook on low for 9 to 10 hours. Turn control to high. Dissolve flour in small amount of cold water; stir into meat mixture. Cook on high 10 to 15 minutes or until slightly thickened. Serve goulash over noodles or rice. Makes 5 to 6 servings.

OLD WORLD SAUERBRATEN

3 1/2 to 4 lbs. beef rump or sirloin tip
1 cup water
1 cup vinegar
1 large onion, sliced
1 lemon, sliced (unpeeled)
10 whole cloves

4 bay leaves
6 whole peppercorns
2 tbs. salt
2 tbs. sugar
12 gingersnaps, crumbled

Place meat in deep ceramic or glass bowl. Combine water, vinegar, onion, lemon, cloves, bay leaves, pepper, salt, and sugar. Pour over meat. Cover and refrigerate for 24 to 36 hours; turn meat several times during marinating. Place beef in slow-cooking pot; pour 1 cup marinade over meat. Cover and cook on low 6 to 8 hours. Place meat on serving platter. Strain meat juices and return to pot. Turn control to high. Stir in gingersnaps; cover and cook on high for 10 to 15 minutes. Pour over meat. Makes 8 servings.

ALPHABET POT ROAST

3 to 4-lb. beef pot roast
Salt and pepper
1 (10 3/4-oz.) can alphabet vegetable soup, undiluted

1/2 cup dry red wine
1/8 tsp. dried basil
2 tbs. finely chopped parsley

Sprinkle beef with salt and pepper. Place in slow-cooking pot. In small mixing bowl, combine undiluted soup with wine and basil. Pour over meat. Cover and cook on low for 8 to 10 hours. Sprinkle with parsley. Slice meat; serve with sauce ladled over meat. (Sauce may be thickened with flour dissolved in a small amount of water, if desired.) Makes 6 to 8 servings.

FAVORITE POT ROAST

3 to 4-lb. beef rump or chuck roast
1 tsp. salt
1/2 tsp. seasoned salt
1/4 tsp. seasoned pepper

1/4 tsp. paprika
1 tbs. instant minced onion
1 cup beef bouillon

Rub all sides of meat with salt, seasoned salt, seasoned pepper, and paprika. In slow-cooking pot, combine seasoned beef with onion and bouillon. Cover and cook on low 8 to 10 hours or until meat is tender. Remove from pot; slice. Makes 6 to 8 servings. If gravy is preferred, thicken juices with flour dissolved in a small amount of water after removing meat from pot. If desired, vegetables such as potatoes, carrots, small white onions, celery, or turnips may be added with bouillon and cooked the same time as meat.

Spicy Wine Pot Roast   Courtesy Cling Peach Advisory Board

SPICY WINE POT ROAST

3 to 4-lb. beef pot roast
Salt and pepper
1 small onion, chopped
1 (3/4-oz.) package brown gravy mix
1 cup water

1/4 cup catsup
1/4 cup dry red wine
2 tsp. Dijon-style mustard
1 tsp. Worcestershire sauce
1/8 tsp. garlic powder

Sprinkle meat with salt and pepper; place in slow-cooking pot. Combine remaining ingredients; pour over meat. Cover and cook on low 8 to 10 hours. Remove meat and slice. If desired thicken sauce with flour dissolved in a small amount of water, and serve over meat. Makes 6 to 7 servings.

Dilled Pot Roast   Courtesy California Beef Council

DILLED POT ROAST

3 to 3 1/2-lb. beef pot roast
1 tsp. salt
1/4 tsp. pepper
1 tsp. dill weed
1/4 cup water

1 tbs. vinegar
3 tbs. flour
1 tsp. dill weed
1 cup dairy sour cream

Sprinkle both sides of meat with salt, pepper, and 1 tsp. dill. Place in slow-cooking pot. Add water and vinegar. Cover and cook on low for 7 to 9 hours or until tender. Remove meat from pot. Turn control to high. Dissolve flour in small amount of cold water; stir into meat drippings. Stir in additional 1 tsp. dill. Cook on high about 10 minutes or until slightly thick. Stir in sour cream; turn off heat. Slice meat; serve with sauce. Makes 6 to 7 servings.

Corned Beef   Courtesy Florida Department of Citrus

CORNED BEEF

3 to 4-lb. corned beef brisket
Water
1/2 cup chopped onion

2 garlic cloves, minced
2 bay leaves
1 head cabbage, cut into wedges (optional)

Place corned beef in slow-cooking pot. Barely cover with water. Add onion, garlic, and bay leaves. Cover and cook on low for 10 to 12 hours. Makes 6 to 8 servings.

If cabbage is desired, lift cooked corned beef out of pot, turn control to high, and drop wedges of cabbage into corned beef broth. Cover and cook 20 to 30 minutes or until cabbage is done.

SPICED BEEF TONGUE

1 (3 to 4-lb.) beef tongue
2 quarts water
6 whole cloves
6 whole black peppercorns

2 tsp. salt
4 bay leaves
1/4 cup vinegar

Combine all ingredients in slow-cooking pot. Cover and cook on low for 10 to 12 hours or until tender. Remove from pot; drain. Cool slightly; remove skin with sharp knife. Serve hot or cold. Slice thinly and serve plain, or with horseradish or mustard sauce. It makes delicious sandwiches when served cold. Makes 8 to 10 servings.

GLAZED CORNED BEEF

3 1/2 to 4-lbs. corned beef
Water
2 tbs. prepared mustard

1 1/2 tsp. horseradish
2 tbs. red wine vinegar
1/4 cup molasses

In slow-cooking pot, cover corned beef with water. Cover and cook on low for 10 to 12 hours. Drain cooked corned beef; place on broiler pan or oven-proof platter. Combine mustard, horseradish, wine vinegar, and molasses. Brush on all sides of meat. Brown in 400° F. oven for about 20 minutes or until it begins to brown; brush with sauce several times while browning. Makes 6 to 8 servings.

Glazed Corned Beef   Courtesy California Beef Council

Lasagne   Photo: Theodore R. Sills. Courtesy National Macaroni Institute

54 Beef

SPICY BRISKET

3 lbs. lean beef brisket
1 tsp. salt
1/4 tsp. pepper
1 sliced onion

1 stalk celery, chopped
1/2 cup chili sauce*
1 can beer

Place beef in slow-cooking pot. Add salt, pepper, onion, celery, and chili sauce. Pour beer over. Cover and cook on low for 8 to 10 hours or until tender. Remove beef from pot; slice. Skim fat off juices; serve juices with meat. Makes 5 to 6 servings.

*Bottled tomato sauce similar to catsup.

SMOKY BRISKET

3 to 4 lbs. lean beef brisket
1 tbs. smoke-flavored salt
2 medium onions, sliced
1 tsp. celery seed

1 tbs. mustard seed
1/2 tsp. pepper
1 (12-oz.) bottle chili sauce (1 cup)

Sprinkle both sides of meat with smoke-flavored salt. Arrange onion slices in bottom of slow-cooking pot. Top with meat. Combine celery seed, mustard seed, pepper, and chili sauce. Pour over meat. Cover and cook on low for 10 to 12 hours or until tender. Makes 8 to 10 servings.

LASAGNE

3/4 lb. lean ground beef
1/2 lb. lean ground pork
1 small onion, chopped
1 clove garlic, minced
1 (16-oz.) can tomatoes, cut up
1 (8-oz.) can tomato sauce
1 beef bouillon cube, crushed
1 tbs. parsley flakes
2 tsp. sugar

1/2 tsp. salt
1/2 tsp. crushed basil
1 pt. cottage cheese (16 oz.)
1/2 cup grated Parmesan cheese
1/2 tsp. salt
1/2 tsp. crushed oregano
8 oz. lasagne noddles, cooked and drained
8 oz. mozzarella cheese, sliced

In large skillet or slow-cooking pot with browning unit, cook and stir beef, pork, onion, and garlic. Drain off excess fat. In slow-cooking pot, combine drained beef, pork, onion, and garlic with tomatoes, tomato sauce, bouillon cube, parsley, sugar, 1/2 tsp. salt, and basil. Cover and cook on low for 6 to 8 hours. Mix cottage cheese, 1/4 cup Parmesan cheese, 1/2 tsp. salt, and oregano. In 13 x 9-inch pan, layer half the cooked noodles, sauce, mozzarella cheese, and cottage cheese mixture; repeat, reserving enough sauce for layer on top. Sprinkle with 1/4 cup grated Parmesan cheese. Bake in 350°F. oven for 45 minutes. Makes 8 to 10 servings.

Italian Pot Roast with added onions, carrots and artichokes   Courtesy California Beef Council

ITALIAN POT ROAST

3 to 4-lb. beef chuck roast
Salt and pepper

1 (1 1/2-oz.) package spaghetti sauce mix
2 tomatoes, chopped

Sprinkle meat with salt and pepper and then dry spaghetti seasoning mix. Place in slow-cooking pot.
Top with chopped tomatoes. Cover and cook on low for 7 to 9 hours or until meat is tender.
Slice and serve on hot spaghetti; spoon sauce over all. Makes 6 to 7 servings.

FONDUE ITALIANO

1 lb. lean ground beef
1 envelope spaghetti sauce mix
2 (15-oz.) cans tomato sauce
1 lb. sharp cheddar cheese, shredded

8 oz. mozzarella cheese, shredded
2 tbs. cornstarch
1/2 cup dry red wine

In skillet or slow-cooking pot with browning unit, cook beef until crumbly; pour off excess fat. In slow-cooking pot, combine beef with dry spaghetti sauce mix, tomato sauce, cheddar and mozzarella cheeses. Cover and cook on low 2 hours. Dissolve cornstarch in wine. Turn control to high. Add dissolved cornstarch. Heat on high for 10 to 15 minutes. Dip chunks of Italian bread into fondue while keeping mixture hot in slow-cooking pot. May be used as a hearty hot dip or as a main dish served with a salad after the game or theatre. Makes 6 to 8 servings.

SPAGHETTI SAUCE

1 lb. lean ground beef
1 large onion, chopped
1 clove garlic, minced
2 (1-lb.) cans tomatoes, cut up
1 (8-oz.) can tomato sauce
1 (12-oz.) can tomato paste
1 cup beef bouillon

2 tbs. minced parsley
1 tbs. brown sugar
1 tsp. dried oregano leaves
1 tsp. dried basil leaves
1 tsp. salt
1/4 tsp. pepper

In large skillet or slow-cooking pot with browning unit, crumble meat with onion and garlic. Break up pieces of meat with fork and cook until it loses its red color. Drain off excess fat. In slow-cooking pot, combine browned meat, onions, and garlic with remaining ingredients. Cover and cook on low for 6 to 8 hours. Serve over hot spaghetti. May be made ahead of time and frozen. Makes 6 to 8 servings.

ITALIAN MEAT BALL STEW

1 1/2 lbs. lean ground beef
1/2 cup fine bread crumbs
2 beaten eggs
1/4 cup milk
2 tbs. grated Parmesan cheese
1 tsp. salt
1/8 tsp. garlic salt
1/4 tsp. pepper
2 carrots, peeled and cut into 1-inch slices

1 (6-oz.) can tomato paste
1 cup water
1 cup beef bouillon
1/2 tsp. oregano
1 tsp. seasoned salt
1/2 tsp. basil
1 (10-oz.) package frozen Italian-style vegetables,
    partially thawed

Combine beef with bread crumbs, eggs, milk, cheese, salt, garlic salt, and pepper. Form into 2-inch balls. Drop carrots in bottom of slow-cooking pot. Arrange meat balls over carrots. Combine tomato paste with water, bouillon, oregano, seasoned salt, and basil. Pour over meat. Cover and cook on low for 4 to 6 hours. Turn to high. Add Italian vegetables. Cover and cook on high for 15 to 20 minutes or until vegetables are tender. Makes 6 servings.

Italian Meat Ball Stew   Courtesy California Beef Council

Spaghetti Sauce with Meatballs Photo: Theodore R. Sills. Courtesy National Macaroni Institute

Festive Meat Balls Courtesy California Beef Council

FESTIVE MEAT BALLS

1 1/2 lbs. lean ground beef
1 (4 1/2-oz.) can deviled ham
2/3 cup evaporated milk
2 eggs, beaten slightly
1 tbs. grated onion
2 cups soft bread crumbs
1/2 tsp. salt

1/4 tsp. allspice
1/4 tsp. pepper
1/4 cup flour
1/4 cup water
1 tbs. catsup
1 tsp. dill weed
1 cup dairy sour cream

Combine beef and ham with milk, eggs, onion, bread crumbs, salt, allspice, and pepper. Shape into meat balls about 2 inches in diameter. (If desired, meat balls may be smaller.) Carefully arrange meat balls in slow-cooking pot. Cover and cook on low for 2 1/2 to 3 1/2 hours. Turn control to high. Stir in flour that has been dissolved in 1/4 cup water. Add catsup and dill weed. Cook on high for 15 to 20 minutes or until slightly thickened. Turn heat off; stir in sour cream. Makes 5 to 7 servings.

BEEFBURGER STROGANOFF

1 1/2 lbs. lean ground beef
3 slices bacon, diced
1 small onion
2 tbs. flour
1/4 tsp. paprika
1 tsp. salt

1 (10 3/4-oz.) can condensed cream of mushroom
  soup
2 tbs. dry red wine
1 cup dairy sour cream
6 to 8 hamburger buns, toasted and buttered

In large skillet or slow-cooking pot with browning unit, brown beef and bacon until red color disappears. Drain. In slow-cooking pot, mix together drained beef, bacon, onion, flour, paprika and salt. Stir in undiluted soup and wine. Cover pot and cook on low 4 to 5 hours. Stir in sour cream. Spoon mixture over toasted buns. For an easy-on-the-cook meal, serve with fresh vegetable relishes and potato chips. Makes 6 to 8 servings.

HAMBURGER SOUP

1 lb. lean ground beef
1/4 tsp. pepper
1/4 tsp. oregano
1/4 tsp. basil
1/4 tsp. seasoned salt
1 envelope onion soup mix
3 cups boiling water

1 (8-oz.) can tomato sauce
1 tbs. soy sauce
1 cup sliced celery
1 cup sliced carrots
1 cup macaroni, cooked and drained
1/4 cup grated Parmesan cheese

Crumble beef into slow-cooking pot. Add pepper, oregano, basil, seasoned salt, and dry soup mix. Stir in water, tomato sauce and soy sauce; then add celery and carrots. Cover and cook on low for 6 to 8 hours. Turn control to high. Add cooked macaroni and Parmesan cheese. Cover and cook on high for 10 to 15 minutes. Makes 5 to 6 servings.

CLARA'S BEEF & POTATOES

2 lbs. lean ground beef
1 tsp. salt
1/2 tsp. pepper
1/4 cup finely chopped onion

1 can condensed tomato soup
5 to 6 medium potatoes
1 cup light cream

In large skillet or slow-cooking pot with browning unit, brown beef; break up large chunks with fork. Pour off excess fat. In small bowl, mix together salt, pepper, onion, and undiluted soup. Peel and slice potatoes. In slow-cooking pot, arrange alternate layers of potatoes and meat (with potatoes on bottom). Pour soup mixture over. Cover and cook on low for 4 to 6 hours. Turn control to high. Pour cream over all; cover and cook on high for 15 to 20 minutes. Makes 6 servings.

SWEDISH CABBAGE ROLLS

12 large cabbage leaves	1 lb. lean ground beef
1 beaten egg	1 cup cooked rice
1/4 cup milk	1 (8-oz.) can tomato sauce
1/4 cup finely chopped onion	1 tbs. brown sugar
1 tsp. salt	1 tbs. lemon juice
1/4 tsp. pepper	1 tsp. Worcestershire sauce

Immerse cabbage leaves in large kettle of boiling water for about 3 minutes or until limp; drain. Combine egg, milk, onion, salt, pepper, beef, and cooked rice. Place about 1/4 cup meat mixture in center of each leaf; fold in sides and roll ends over meat. Place in slow-cooking pot. Combine tomato sauce with brown sugar, lemon juice, and Worcestershire sauce. Pour over cabbage rolls. Cover and cook on low 7 to 9 hours. Makes 6 servings.

1/Place about 1/4 cup meat mixture in center of each cabbage leaf.

2/Fold in cabbage leaf sides and roll ends over meat.

3/Place cabbage rolls in slow-cooking pot. Pour tomato sauce over cabbage rolls.

CHEESY MEAT LOAF

16 to 18 round cheese crackers
1 small onion, finely chopped
2 tbs. minced green pepper
1/4 cup chili sauce*
1/2 cup milk

2 eggs, slightly beaten
3/4 tsp. salt
1/8 tsp. pepper
1 1/2 lbs. lean ground beef

Crush crackers with rolling pin or blender until crumbled. In mixing bowl, combine crumbs with onion, green pepper, chili sauce, milk, eggs, salt, and pepper. Mix in ground beef. Form into 6 or 7-inch round loaf. Place in slow-cooking pot. Cover and cook on low for 6 to 8 hours or until done. Makes 6 to 8 servings.

*Bottled tomato sauce similar to catsup.

ITALIAN BEEF & POTATO CASSEROLE

1 lb. lean ground beef
1 (5 1/2-oz.) pkg. scalloped potatoes
1 (16-oz.) can tomatoes
1 (10 1/2-oz.) can pizza sauce
1/2 cup water
1/2 tsp. salt

1/2 tsp. oregano leaves
1/4 tsp. basil leaves
1/8 tsp. garlic powder
1 cup mozzarella cheese, cut into small cubes
1/4 cup grated Parmesan cheese

In skillet or slow-cooking pot with browning unit, brown meat until crumbly; drain off fat. In slow-cooking pot, combine beef with dry sauce mix from package of scalloped potatoes, tomatoes, pizza sauce, water, salt, oregano, basil and garlic powder. Stir in dry potato slices. Cover and cook on low 4 to 5 hours. Turn control to high. Stir in cubes of mozzarella cheese. Top with Parmesan cheese. Cover and cook on high for 10 to 15 minutes. Makes 4 to 6 servings.

STUFFED GREEN PEPPERS

5 to 6 green peppers
1/2 lb. lean ground beef
1/4 cup finely chopped onion
1 tbs. chopped pimiento
1 tsp. salt

1 (12-oz.) can whole kernel corn, drained
1 tbs. Worcestershire sauce
1 tsp. prepared mustard
1 (10 3/4-oz.) can condensed cream of tomato soup

Cut a slice off top of each pepper. Remove core, seeds, and white membrane. In small bowl, combine beef, onion, pimiento, salt, and corn. Spoon into peppers. Stand peppers up in slow-cooking pot. Add Worcestershire sauce and mustard to soup. Pour over peppers. Cover pot; cook on low 8 to 10 hours. Makes 5 to 6 servings.

FAMILY FAVORITE MEAT LOAF

2 beaten eggs
3/4 cup milk
2/3 cup fine dry bread crumbs
2 tbs. grated onion

1 tsp. salt
1/2 tsp. ground sage
1 1/2 lbs. ground beef

Sauce:
1/4 cup catsup
2 tbs. brown sugar

1 tsp. dry mustard
1/4 tsp. ground nutmeg

Combine eggs with milk, bread crumbs, onion, salt, sage, and meat. Mix well and shape into 9 x 5-inch rectangle or oval, or about 6-inch round. Carefully place in slow-cooking pot. Cook on low for 5 to 6 hours. Combine sauce ingredients in small bowl; pour over meat. Cover and cook on high 15 minutes longer. Slice and serve while hot or use cold slices for sandwiches. Makes 6 servings.

Shape meat loaf to fit bottom of your slow-cooking pot. Carefully place loaf on bottom of pot.

Short-Cut Chili Con Carne   Courtesy California Dry Bean Advisory Board

SHORT-CUT CHILI CON CARNE

1 lb. lean ground beef
1 small onion, chopped
1 tsp. salt
1 to 2 tsp. chili powder

1 bay leaf
1 tsp. Worcestershire sauce
2 (8-oz.) cans tomato sauce
2 (16-oz.) cans kidney beans, drained

In skillet or slow-cooking pot with browning unit, break up beef with fork and cook until lightly browned. Pour off excess fat. In slow-cooking pot, combine meat with onion, salt, chili powder, bay leaf, Worcestershire sauce, tomato sauce, and kidney beans. Cover and cook on high for 2 to 3 hours. Remove bay leaf. Makes 6 to 7 servings.

OTHER MEATS

When it comes to a choice of meats for your pot, the sky is the limit. Use your slow-cooking pot as an excuse for trying some of those meats you've seen at the market and always intended to buy. Or, use it for variations of old favorites. This way you can add new variety to your menus without wiping out the budget!

Be sure to check the meat at the minimum suggested cooking time. Let it cook longer if necessary to suit your own taste buds. With a little experience you will develop a "feel" for the time needed for the exact degree of done-ness you like.

Meat recipes combined with vegetables will keep your meat-hungry family happy while allowing you to stay out of the kitchen until the last few minutes before dinner.

Some larger roasts are designed to fit into 4 1/2-quart and larger cookers. You may want to use a meat thermometer with these just as you would when cooking in the oven. If yours is a 3 1/2-quart or smaller pot, use a small size roast and/or have the butcher remove any bones and tie the meat to make it more compact. Remember: Smaller roasts take slightly less cooking time.

You will have more meat juices when you finish than you get with other cooking methods. Make the most of the wonderful flavor these juices contain by spooning them over slices of the meat, or thickening them with dissolved flour or cornstarch. Pass the gravy to serve over rice, potatoes or noodles.

Pork—To brown or not to brown—that is the question. It's a good idea to brown spareribs before cooking them in a slow-cooking pot. Lightly brown them in the oven and drain the excess fat before adding sauce and vegetables. If pork steaks and chops are fairly lean, either brown them, or just trim the excess fat off the edges.

Lamb—The same principle applies to lamb. If there is fat, trim off the excess or brown it and drain off the fat before placing it in your slow-cooking pot. You may want to pour off the fat at least once during the cooking process.

GOURMET LEG OF LAMB

1 (5 to 6-lb.) leg of lamb*
1 clove garlic
1/4 cup Kosher or coarse salt

2 tbs. peppercorns, cracked
1/4 cup cognac or brandy
2 cups dry red wine

Trim excess fat from lamb. Cut garlic clove into 4 to 6 slices. Using a paring knife, make enough small slits to insert slivers of garlic into various parts of meat. Sprinkle coarse salt and pepper over all sides of lamb. Place in large bowl; pour cognac or brandy over it. Refrigerate several hours or overnight, brushing with cognac or brandy and turning meat several times. Drain meat and put it and red wine in slow-cooking pot. Cover and cook on low 10 to 12 hours or until meat is done. If possible, turn roast in pot once during cooking. Makes 8 to 10 servings.

*This recipe designed for a 4 1/2 quart or larger slow-cooking pot. Have your butcher bone the leg of lamb to fit into a smaller pot.

HERBED LEG OF LAMB

4 1/2 to 5 1/2-lb. leg of lamb*
1 clove garlic, peeled and halved
1 tbs. dry mustard
1 tsp. salt
1/8 tsp. pepper

1/2 tsp. thyme leaves
1/4 tsp. crushed rosemary leaves
1 tbs. lemon juice
1/4 cup flour

Rub all surfaces of lamb with garlic. Mix mustard with salt, pepper, thyme, rosemary and lemon juice. Spread and pat herb mixture on surface of roast. Place roast on metal rack in slow-cooking pot. Cover pot and cook on low for 10 to 12 hours or until tender. Remove meat to platter. Skim off excess fat from juices. Turn control to high. Dissolve flour in small amount of cold water. Stir into juices in pot. Cook on high for 15 to 20 minutes. Serve herbed sauce with meat. Makes 8 to 10 servings.

*This recipe designed for a 4 1/2 quart or larger slow-cooking pot. If you have a smaller pot, ask the butcher to bone the leg of lamb or buy a smaller one.

SPICY LAMB SHANKS

4 to 5 lamb shanks*
1 tsp. salt
1/4 tsp. pepper
1 cup dried apricots
1 cup pitted prunes
1 cup water

2 tbs. vinegar
1/3 cup sugar
1/2 tsp. ground allspice
1/2 tsp. ground cinnamon
1/4 tsp. ground cloves

Coat lamb shanks with salt and pepper. Place in slow-cooking pot. Add apricots and prunes. Combine water and vinegar with sugar, allspice, cinnamon, and cloves. Pour over fruits and meat. Cover and cook on low for 7 to 9 hours or until meat is tender. Makes 4 to 5 servings.

*Four lamb shanks fit into 3 1/2 qt. slow-cooking pot; a larger pot is needed for more than 4 shanks.

IRISH LAMB STEW

1 1/2 lbs. lamb, cut into 2-inch cubes
1 tbs. shortening
2 medium onions, chopped
4 cups beef broth
3 medium potatoes, peeled and thinly sliced
1/2 tsp. salt

1/4 tsp. pepper
1/4 tsp. celery seed
1/4 tsp. marjoram leaves, crushed
1/8 tsp. thyme leaves, crushed
1 (10-oz.) package frozen peas, partially thawed
6 tbs. flour

In large skillet or slow-cooking pot with browning unit, brown meat in shortening. Combine browned meat in slow-cooking pot with remaining ingredients except peas and flour. Cover and cook on low for 8 to 10 hours or until meat and potatoes are done. Add peas; then flour dissolved in 1/2 cup cold water. Turn control to high; cover and cook on high 15 to 20 minutes. Makes 5 to 6 servings.

AUTUMN PORK CHOPS

6 pork chops
2 medium acorn squash, unpeeled
3/4 tsp. salt
2 tbs. melted butter or margarine

3/4 cup brown sugar, packed
3/4 tsp. brown bouquet sauce
1 tbs. orange juice
1/2 tsp. grated orange peel

Trim excess fat from chops. Cut each squash into 4 to 5 crosswise slices; remove seeds. Arrange 3 chops on bottom of slow-cooking pot. Place all squash slices on top; then another layer of remaining 3 chops. Combine salt, butter, sugar, bouquet sauce, orange juice, and orange peel. Spoon over chops. Cover and cook on low for 4 to 6 hours or until done. Serve one or two slices of squash with each pork chop. Makes 6 servings.

GOLDEN GLOW PORK CHOPS

5 to 6 pork chops
1/4 cup brown sugar
1/2 tsp. ground cinnamon
1/4 tsp. ground cloves

1 (8-oz.) can tomato sauce
1 (29-oz.) can cling peach halves
1/4 cup vinegar
Salt and pepper

Lightly brown pork chops on both sides in large skillet or slow-cooking pot with browning unit. Pour off excess fat. Combine brown sugar, cinnamon, cloves, tomato sauce, 1/4 cup syrup from peaches, and vinegar. Sprinkle chops with salt and pepper. Arrange chops in slow-cooking pot. Place drained peach halves on top. Pour tomato mixture over all. Cover and cook on low for 4 to 6 hours. Makes 5 to 6 servings.

Fruited Pork Chops   Courtesy Cling Peach Advisory Board

FRUITED PORK CHOPS

4 lean pork chops	1/8 tsp. dried dill weed
1/2 tsp. salt	1 (17-oz.) can fruit cocktail
Dash of pepper	2 tbs. cornstarch
1 tbs. prepared mustard	2 tbs. cold water
2 tbs. wine vinegar	

Sprinkle chops with salt and pepper. Place in slow-cooking pot. Combine mustard, vinegar and dill. Drain fruit cocktail; add 1/2 cup syrup from fruit to mustard mixture. Pour over chops in pot. Cover pot and cook on low for 4 to 6 hours or until meat is tender. Remove chops and turn control to high. Dissolve cornstarch in water; stir into pot. Add drained fruit cocktail, cover and cook on high for 10 to 15 minutes. Spoon fruit sauce over chops. Makes 4 servings.

CORN-STUFFED PORK CHOPS

5 to 6 pork chops, 1 to 2 inches thick
1 (7-oz.) can whole kernel corn, not drained
1 cup soft bread crumbs
1 tbs. instant minced onion

2 tbs. minced green pepper
1 tsp. salt
1/2 tsp. sage

Have butcher cut a pocket or with a sharp knife cut a horizontal slit in side of each chop forming a pocket for stuffing. Mix undrained corn, bread crumbs, onion, pepper, salt, and sage. Spoon corn mixture into slits. Close with toothpicks or small skewers. Place on metal rack or trivet in slow-cooking pot. Cover and cook on low for 6 to 8 hours. Especially good with fruit salad and lemon-buttered broccoli. Makes 5 to 6 servings.

PLANTATION PORK CHOPS

4 double cut loin pork chops
2 cups corn bread stuffing mix
2 tbs. melted butter or margarine
1/4 tsp. salt
1/3 cup orange juice

1 tbs. finely chopped pecans
Salt and pepper
1/4 cup light corn syrup
1/2 tsp. grated orange peel

Have butcher cut a pocket or with a sharp knife cut a horizontal slit in side of each chop forming a pocket for stuffing. Combine stuffing with butter, 1/4 tsp. salt, orange juice, and pecans. Fill pockets with stuffing. Sprinkle chops with salt and pepper. Place on metal rack in slow-cooking pot. Brush with mixture of corn syrup and orange peel. Cover and cook on low for 6 to 8 hours. Uncover; turn control to high and brush with sauce again. Cook on high for 15 to 20 minutes. Makes 4 servings.

1/Fill pork chop pockets with stuffing.

2/Place on metal rack or trivet in slow-cooking pot. Brush with mixture of corn syrup and orange peel.

NORTH-OF-THE-BORDER POZOLE

4 pork steaks
Salt and pepper
1 (14 1/2-oz.) can hominy, drained

1 small onion, chopped
1 (4-oz.) can diced green chili peppers, drained
1 tsp. chili powder

Trim fat off pork steaks; sprinkle with salt and pepper. Combine hominy with onion, chili peppers, and chili powder in bottom of slow-cooking pot. Arrange pork steaks over hominy. Cover and cook on low for 4 to 6 hours. Makes 4 servings.

RATHSKELLER PORK

4 to 5 pork steaks, about 3/4 inch thick
1 tbs. salad oil
1 (10 1/2-oz.) can condensed cream of
  asparagus soup
1/2 cup chopped green onions
1 1/2 tsp. seasoned salt

1/2 tsp. seasoned pepper
1/4 cup water
4 potatoes, sliced
2 cups shredded cabbage
1/2 cup light cream

In large skillet or slow-cooking pot with browning unit, brown chops in oil on both sides. Drain off excess fat. Combine undiluted soup with onions, seasoned salt, pepper and water. Arrange alternate layers of meat, potatoes and cabbage in slow-cooking pot. Pour soup mixture over. Cover and cook 4 to 6 hours on low. Turn to high. Add cream; cover and cook on high for 20 to 30 minutes. Makes 4 to 5 servings.

CRANBERRY PORK ROAST

3 to 4-lb. pork roast*
Salt and pepper
1 cup ground or finely chopped cranberries
1/4 cup honey

1 tsp. grated orange peel
1/8 tsp. ground cloves
1/8 tsp. ground nutmeg

Sprinkle roast with salt and pepper. Place in slow-cooking pot. Combine remaining ingredients; pour over roast. Cover and cook on low for 8 to 10 hours. Makes 6 to 8 servings.

*Boneless or pork loin roast may be used.

HERBED PORK ROAST

1 (4 to 7-lb.) fresh ham or pork leg*
2 cups water
1 tsp. salt
1 tsp. thyme, crumbled

1 tsp. ground sage
1 tsp. grated lemon peel
1 tbs. lemon juice
1 clove garlic

Remove skin and excess fat from pork. Place in large bowl. Pour water over; add remaining ingredients. Cover and refrigerate several hours or overnight. Turn meat two or three times if possible. Transfer meat and marinade to slow-cooking pot. Cover and cook on low for 10 to 12 hours or until meat is done. If possible, turn meat in pot once during cooking. Drain and slice. Makes 8 servings.

*The larger roast fits a 4 1/2 quart or larger slow-cooking pot. If you have a smaller slow-cooking pot, have the butcher bone the roast or buy a smaller one.

INDONESIAN PORK

1 (4 to 5-lb.) pork roast
Salt and pepper
1 cup hot water
1/4 cup molasses

1/4 cup prepared mustard
1/4 cup vinegar
1/4 cup orange marmalade
1/4 tsp. ground ginger

Place metal rack or trivet in bottom of slow-cooking pot. Sprinkle pork roast with salt and pepper; put on trivet in pot. Pour hot water around pork roast. Cover and cook on low for 8 to 10 hours or until done. Remove meat from pot. Place on broiler pan or oven-proof platter. Combine molasses, mustard, vinegar, marmalade, and ginger. Brush over cooked pork. Brown in 400°F. oven for 30 minutes, brushing several times with sauce. Makes 6 to 8 servings.

SWEET-SOUR SPARERIBS

3 to 4 lbs. spareribs
Salt and pepper
1 cup chicken bouillon
1/4 cup brown sugar
1/4 cup vinegar

1 tbs. soy sauce
1 small onion, thinly sliced
2 tbs. cornstarch
1 (11-oz.) can mandarin oranges, drained
1 medium green pepper, cut into chunks

Cut spareribs into serving-size pieces. Sprinkle with salt and pepper. Place on rack in shallow baking pan. Roast in 400°F. oven for 15 minutes. Turn and brown other side. Drain fat and put ribs in slow-cooking pot. Combine bouillon with brown sugar, vinegar, and soy sauce. Pour over ribs in pot. Cover and cook on low for 6 to 8 hours. Turn control to high. Add onion. Dissolve cornstarch in small amount of cold water; stir into pot. Cover and cook on high another 10 to 15 minutes or until slightly thickened. Stir in oranges and green pepper. Cover and cook 5 minutes. Serve over cooked rice or crisp Chinese noodles. Makes 4 to 6 servings.

CHINESE STYLE COUNTRY RIBS

1/4 cup soy sauce
1/4 cup orange marmalade
2 tbs. catsup

1 clove garlic, crushed
3 to 4 lbs. country-style spareribs*

Combine soy sauce, marmalade, catsup, and garlic. Brush on both sides of ribs. Place in slow-cooking pot. Pour remaining sauce over all. Cover and cook on low for 8 to 10 hours. Makes 4 to 6 servings.

*Also known as farm-style ribs. Regular spareribs may be substituted.

Soy-Glazed Spareribs   Courtesy National Livestock & Meat Board

SOY-GLAZED SPARERIBS

4 to 5 lbs. spareribs, cut into two-rib pieces
Salt and pepper
1/2 cup pineapple juice
2 tbs. garlic-flavored wine vinegar
1/4 cup dry white wine

2 tbs. soy sauce
2 tbs. honey
1/2 cup chicken broth or bouillon
2 tbs. cornstarch
3 tbs. cold water

Place spareribs on rack in shallow baking pan. Brown in 400°F. oven for 30 minutes, turning ribs once. Remove from oven; pour off fat. Sprinkle ribs with salt and pepper. Place in slow-cooking pot. Combine remaining ingredients except cornstarch and water; pour over ribs. Cover and cook on low 7 to 9 hours. Turn control to high. Dissolve cornstarch in 3 tbs. cold water. Stir into rib mixture. Cook 10 to 15 minutes or until slightly thickened. Makes 5 to 6 servings.

Indonesian Pork   Courtesy United Fresh Fruit and Vegetable Association

BUCK'S COUNTY SPARERIBS

2 1/2 to 3 lbs. spareribs
1 tsp. salt
1/4 tsp. pepper

1 (1-lb.) can sauerkraut, drained
1 apple, cored and diced (with peel)
1 tbs. sugar

Cut spareribs into serving-size pieces. Sprinkle with salt and pepper. Place on rack in baking pan. Brown in 400°F. oven for 15 minutes; turn and brown on other side (about 10 or 15 minutes). Pour off drippings. Spoon sauerkraut into bottom of slow-cooking pot. Top with apple, sprinkle sugar over the apple, and put the ribs on top. Cover pot and cook on low for 6 to 8 hours or until meat is tender. Makes 4 servings.

BARBECUED SPARERIBS

4 to 5 lbs. spareribs, cut into two-rib pieces
1/2 cup catsup
2 tbs. brown sugar
1/2 cup bottled steak sauce

2 tbs. vinegar
1/4 tsp. salt
1/2 tsp. hickory smoke salt
1 tsp. instant minced onion

Place spareribs on rack in baking pan. Brown in 400°F. oven for 15 minutes; turn and brown on other side for 10 or 15 minutes. Drain fat and put ribs in slow-cooking pot. Combine remaining ingredients; pour over ribs. Cover and cook on low 6 to 8 hours. Makes 5 to 6 servings.

ALL-PURPOSE BARBECUE SAUCE

1 cup catsup
1 tbs. Worcestershire sauce
2 or 3 drops bottled hot pepper sauce
1 cup water
1/4 cup vinegar

1 tbs. brown sugar
1 tsp. salt
1 tsp. celery seed
1 tbs. instant minced onion

Combine ingredients in slow-cooking pot. Cover and cook on low 2 to 3 hours. Makes 2 to 2 1/4 cups sauce. Good on spareribs, chicken, pork chops, sliced roast beef.

Crockery Ham   Courtesy Cling Peach Advisory Board

CROCKERY HAM

5 to 7-lb. cooked ham (with or without
   bone, butt or shank half)*
Whole cloves
1/2 cup currant jelly

1 tbs. vinegar
1/2 tsp. dry mustard
1/4 tsp. ground cinnamon

Place ham on metal rack or trivet in slow-cooking pot. Cover and cook on low 5 to 6 hours.
Remove ham. Pour off juices; remove rind. Score ham; stud with whole cloves. In small saucepan,
melt jelly with remaining ingredients. Remove metal rack or trivet. Return meat to slow-cooking pot.
Spoon sauce over ham. Cover pot and cook on high for 20 to 30 minutes, brushing with sauce at
least once (several times if possible). Makes 8 to 10 servings.

*The larger cuts of ham fit in a 4 1/2 quart or larger slow-cooking pot. If you own a smaller pot,
substitute a boneless ham.

HAM AND CHICKEN PIE

1 (10 3/4-oz.) can condensed cream of mush-
    room soup
1/8 tsp. marjoram
1/8 tsp. thyme
1/4 cup chopped onion
1/2 cup chopped celery
1 (2 1/2-oz.) can mushrooms, drained

1 cup diced cooked ham
1 cup diced cooked chicken
1 (10-oz.) package frozen peas, thawed
1 (8-oz.) package refrigerator biscuits
Melted butter
1 tbs. sesame seeds

In large bowl, combine soup with marjoram, thyme, onion, celery, mushrooms, ham, chicken, and peas. Pour into slow-cooking pot. Cover and cook on low for 5 to 6 hours. Spoon into shallow baking dish.* Arrange biscuits on top; brush with melted butter; sprinkle with sesame seeds. Bake in 350°F. oven for 20 to 25 minutes or until biscuits are brown. Makes 4 to 5 servings.

*Ham and chicken mixture may be refrigerated at this point, then topped with biscuits and baked just before serving time.

HOMESTEAD HAM LOAF

1 lb. ground cooked ham (about 3 cups)
1/2 lb. lean bulk sausage
1 cup dry bread crumbs
1 tbs. prepared mustard

1 egg, beaten
1 tsp. grated onion
1/2 cup milk

Sauce:
1/4 cup brown sauce
1/2 tsp. dry mustard

2 tbs. orange juice

In mixing bowl, combine ham, sausage, bread crumbs, mustard, egg, onion, and milk. Form into round loaf about 6 inches in diameter, or rectangle or oval about 9 x 5 inches. Place in slow-cooking pot. Cover and cook on low for about 7 hours. Combine ingredients for sauce; brush over loaf the last 30 minutes of cooking. Slice and serve hot. Leftover cold slices of loaf make good sandwiches. Makes 6 servings.

CASSOULET EN POT

1/2 lb. bulk pork sausage
1 small onion, sliced
1 clove garlic, minced
2 tbs. minced parsley

2 (15-oz.) cans black-eyed peas, not drained
1/2 lb. cooked ham, cubed
1/4 cup dry white wine

In skillet or slow-cooking pot with browning unit, cook sausage until lightly browned. Pour off excess fat. In slow-cooking pot, arrange alternate layers of sausage, onion, garlic, parsley, black-eyed peas, and ham. Pour wine over all. Cover and cook on low for 5 to 7 hours. Mixture is quite soupy, so serve in bowls. To make a complete meal, add corn muffins and a big green salad. Makes 6 servings.

KNOCKWURST WITH HOT GERMAN POTATO SALAD

4 large potatoes
1 onion, sliced
1 tsp. salt
Water
4 slices bacon, diced
2 tbs. flour
2 tbs. sugar
1 tsp. dry mustard

1 tsp. salt
1/4 tsp. pepper
1/3 cup vinegar
2/3 cup water
1/2 tsp. celery seeds
4 knockwurst links
1 tbs. finely chopped parsley

Peel and slice potatoes. Combine with onion in slow-cooking pot. Sprinkle with 1 tsp. salt. Cover with water. Cover and cook on low for 5 to 6 hours or on high for 2 to 3 hours. Remove from pot; drain thoroughly and return to pot. In the meantime, cook bacon in skillet. Stir in flour, sugar, mustard, 1 tsp. salt, and pepper; mix well. Add vinegar, 2/3 cup water, and celery seeds. Cook several minutes or until thickened. Pour over cooked drained potatoes in slow-cooking pot. Top with knockwurst. Turn control to high. Cover and cook on high for 30 to 40 minutes or until mixture is hot. Sprinkle with parsley. Makes 4 servings.

KNOCKWURST & CABBAGE

5 to 6 knockwurst links
1 onion, thinly sliced
1 small head cabbage, coarsely shredded

1/2 tsp. salt
1 tsp. caraway seeds
2 cups chicken bouillon

Cut knockwurst into 2-inch chunks. In slow-cooking pot, arrange alternate layers of meat* with onions and cabbage. Sprinkle with salt and caraway seeds. Pour bouillon over all. Cover and cook on low 5 to 6 hours or until cabbage is tender. Makes 6 servings.

*If a more chewy texture in the knockwurst is preferred, meat may be added the last hour of cooking.

POULTRY

Nationality favorites from around the world are represented by the variety of poultry dishes you can create in your slow cooker. Elegant *Chicken Breasts, Saltimbocca Style* competes with *Imperial Duckling* and *Stuffed Turkey Breasts* as glamourous company candidates.

While there seems to be an unlimited variation of family favorites, whole chicken, broiler halves or quarters, cut-up chicken parts or cooked chunks of chicken are equally delicious in a slow cooker. Naturally, the larger whole birds require longer cooking time than the bite-size pieces. As a general rule, chicken does not take as long to cook as beef, pork or lamb. Check it for yourself.

Sometimes vegetables take longer to cook than chicken when using carrots, eggplant, celery, or potatoes in a chicken dish. Be sure the vegetables are covered with liquid such as water, bouillon or tomato sauce. Also, you may want to place the vegetables on the bottom of the pot with the chicken on top. This way, the vegetables cook more evenly and should be done about the same time as the chicken.

Duckling requires special attention because of its excess fat. When cooking duck, be sure to stick it with a fork at 2-inch intervals. Place it on a metal rack or trivet in the bottom of your slow cooker so the fat can drip to the bottom. Then pour off the fat at least once during the cooking.

For a change of pace, you'll like the way turkey parts taste when slow-cooked. Turkey legs, thighs, and wings lend themselves especially well to this cooking method. They are tender, juicy and most flavorful. Larger turkey parts fit into 4 1/2-quart or larger pots. If you have a 3 1/2-quart pot, buy the smaller parts or remove the bones so the turkey will fit.

Turkey loaf is a shapely new version of the ever-popular family favorite, meat loaf. Try one and you'll have everyone guessing. Shape it in a loaf or oval, depending on the size of your slow cooker.

Chicken Marengo   Photo: Josh Young

CHICKEN MARENGO

2 1/2 to 3-lb. frying chicken, cut up
1 (1 1/2-oz.) package spaghetti sauce mix
1/2 cup dry white wine

2 fresh tomatoes, quartered
1/4 lb. fresh mushrooms

Place chicken parts in bottom of slow-cooking pot. Combine dry spaghetti sauce mix with wine; pour over chicken. Cover and cook on low 6 to 7 hours. Turn control to high. Add tomatoes and mushrooms. Cover and cook on high for 30 to 40 minutes or until tomatoes are done. Makes 4 to 5 servings.

MISSION CHICKEN

2 (2 1/2-lb.) broiler-fryers, quartered
1/4 cup butter
1/4 tsp. ground cinnamon
1/4 tsp. ground cloves
1 tsp. salt
1 tsp. seasoned salt

1 (6-oz.) can frozen orange juice concentrate, thawed
1/2 cup water
2 or 3 drops hot pepper sauce
1 cup seedless grapes, halved
1/2 cup slivered, toasted almonds

In large skillet or slow-cooking pot with browning unit, brown chicken in butter. Combine cinnamon, cloves, salt, seasoned salt, orange juice concentrate, water, and hot pepper sauce. Pour this mixture over chicken in slow-cooking pot. Cover and cook on low for 4 to 5 hours or until chicken is tender. Stir in grapes. Place chicken in serving dish; sprinkle with almonds. If preferred, pass sauce in separate bowl or thicken with flour dissolved in a small amount of water. Makes 8 servings.

CHICKEN SESAME

1 frying chicken, cut up
1/4 cup flour
3 tbs. sesame seeds
1/2 tsp. salt
1/4 tsp. pepper
1/4 cup salad oil
1 small onion, chopped

2 stalks celery, chopped
1/2 cup dry white wine
1 chicken bouillon cube, crumbled
1/2 tsp. tarragon
1/4 cup cornstarch
1/4 cup water
1 cup dairy sour cream

Coat chicken with mixture of flour, sesame seeds, salt, and pepper. In large skillet or slow-cooking pot with browning unit, brown chicken in oil. Add onion, celery, wine, bouillon cube, and tarragon. Cover and cook on low 6 to 8 hours. Turn control to high. Remove chicken to warm shallow dish. Dissolve cornstarch in water and stir into pot. Cook on high 15 minutes. Turn heat off; stir in sour cream. Pour sauce over chicken; serve hot. Makes 5 servings. Especially good with hot rice.

KOWLOON CHICKEN

3 to 3 1/2 lbs. chicken parts (or cut-up fryer)
Salt and pepper
1/4 tsp. ground ginger
1 clove garlic, minced
1 cup chicken broth or bouillon
1 (8 1/2-oz.) can pineapple slices

1 (4-oz.) can water chestnuts, drained and sliced
4 green onions, diagonally sliced
1/4 cup cornstarch
1/4 cup soy sauce
1 tbs. vinegar

Sprinkle chicken with salt and pepper. Place in slow-cooking pot. Combine ginger, garlic, broth and syrup from pineapple. Cut pineapple slices into fourths. Arrange pineapple and water chestnuts over chicken. Pour ginger sauce over all. Cover and cook on low for 3 to 4 hours or until chicken is tender. Add green onions. Dissolve cornstarch in soy sauce and vinegar. Stir into pot. Cover and cook on high for 10 to 15 minutes or until slightly thickened. Serve with crisp Chinese noodles. Makes 5 to 6 servings.

CHICKEN KONA

3 to 4 lbs. frying chicken parts or 2 small
  broilers, quartered
Salt and pepper
1/2 cup chopped green onion

1/2 cup soy sauce
1/4 cup dry white wine
1/2 cup water
1/2 cup honey

Sprinkle chicken with salt and pepper. Place in slow-cooking pot. Combine onions, soy sauce, wine, and water. Pour over chicken. Cover and cook on low for 3 to 4 hours or until chicken is tender. Remove chicken from pot.* Arrange on broiler pan. Brush honey on chicken. Broil until golden brown, brushing with honey several times. Makes 6 to 8 servings.

*Chicken and sauce may be refrigerated and browned at a later time, if desired.

Curried Chicken   Courtesy Cling Peach Advisory Board and California Prune Advisory Board

CURRIED CHICKEN

1 (2 1/2 to 3 1/2-lb.) chicken fryer, cut up
Salt and pepper
1 tbs. curry powder
1 clove garlic, crushed
1 tbs. melted butter
1/2 cup chicken bouillon

1 tbs. instant minced onion
1 (29-oz.) can cling peach halves
1/2 cup pitted prunes
3 tbs. cornstarch
3 tbs. cold water

Sprinkle chicken with salt and pepper. Place in slow-cooking pot. Combine curry with garlic, butter, bouillon and onion. Drain peaches, saving syrup. Add 1/2 cup peach syrup to curry mixture. Pour curry sauce over chicken. Cover pot and cook on low for 4 to 6 hours. Remove chicken from pot. Turn control to high. Stir in prunes. Dissolve cornstarch in water; stir into sauce in pot. Cover and cook on high for 10 to 15 minutes or until slightly thickened. Add peaches. Serve chicken with sauce. Peanuts, coconut and chutney are ideal accompaniments to this dish. Makes 4 to 5 servings.

CREOLE CHICKEN

1 broiler-fryer chicken, cut up
1 green pepper, chopped
6 green onions, chopped
1 (16-oz.) can tomatoes, cut up
1 (6-oz.) can tomato paste

1/4 lb. cooked ham, cubed (about 3/4 cup)
1 tsp. salt
Several drops bottled hot pepper sauce
1/2 lb. smoked or Polish sausage, sliced
3 cups cooked rice

In slow-cooking pot, combine chicken, pepper, onions, tomatoes, tomato paste, ham, salt and pepper sauce. Cover and cook on low for 4 to 5 hours. Turn control to high. Add sausage and cooked rice. Cover and cook on high for 15 to 20 minutes. Makes 6 to 7 servings.

ARROZ CON POLLO

1 frying chicken, cut up
1 tsp. salt
1/4 tsp. pepper
1 clove garlic, minced
1/16 tsp. saffron powder

3 cups chicken broth or bouillon
2 tbs. dry sherry
1 (16-oz.) can peas, drained
1/2 cup sliced, stuffed green olives
2 cups cooked rice

In slow-cooking pot, combine chicken with salt, pepper, garlic and saffron. Pour chicken broth and sherry over chicken. Cover and cook on low for 4 to 6 hours. Drain chicken; save 2 cups of the broth. Turn control to high. In slow-cooking pot, combine chicken, 2 cups broth, peas, olives, and cooked rice. Cover and cook on high another 20 to 30 minutes, or until hot. Makes 4 to 6 servings.

CHICKEN OLÉ

12 tortillas, cut into 6 or 8 pieces each
4 cups coarsely chopped cooked chicken
    or turkey
1 (10 3/4-oz.) can condensed cream of
    chicken soup

1 (10 3/4-oz.) can condensed cream of mushroom
    soup
1 (7-oz.) can green chili salsa
1 cup dairy sour cream
1 tbs. grated onion
1 1/2 cups grated cheddar cheese

Lightly grease sides and bottom of slow-cooking pot. Arrange alternate layers of tortillas with chicken and mixture of undiluted soups, salsa, sour cream, and onion. Cover and cook on low 4 to 5 hours. Sprinkle with cheese and cook on low another 15 or 20 minutes. Serve with orange and avocado salad, plus additional warm tortillas. Makes 8 servings.

Creole Chicken   Courtesy The McIlhenny Company

AMERICANIZED CHICKEN CHOP SUEY

2 whole chicken breasts, skinned, halved, and boned
1 tsp. salt
1 tsp. minced crystallized ginger
1 cup sliced celery
1 (5-oz.) can water chestnuts, drained and sliced

1 onion, sliced
2 cups chicken bouillon
2 tbs. soy sauce
1 cup sliced mushrooms
1 (1-lb.) can bean sprouts, drained
Cooked rice
1/2 cup slivered almonds

Cut chicken into strips about 2 inches long and 1/2 inch thick. Place in slow-cooking pot with salt, ginger, celery, water chestnuts, onion, bouillon, and soy sauce. Cover and cook on low 5 to 6 hours. Turn control to high. Add mushrooms and bean sprouts. Cover and cook on high 15 minutes. Serve over hot rice. Sprinkle with almonds. Serve with extra soy sauce, if desired. Makes 4 to 6 servings.

NUTTY CHICKEN BREAST

1/4 cup peanut butter
2 tbs. chopped peanuts
2 tbs. soy sauce
1 tbs. instant minced onion
1 tbs. minced parsley
1 clove garlic, crushed
Several drops red pepper sauce
1/8 tsp. ground ginger

4 whole chicken breasts, halved, skinned and boned
2 tbs. soy sauce
2 tbs. honey
1 tbs. melted butter or margarine
1 (10 1/2-oz.) can chicken broth
1 tbs. cornstarch

Mix peanut butter, peanuts, 2 tbs. soy sauce, onion, parsley, garlic, pepper sauce, and ginger. Spread on inside of each chicken breast. Fold in half; close with small skewer or a toothpick. Place in slow-cooking pot. Mix remaining 2 tbs. soy sauce with honey, butter, and broth; pour over chicken. Cover and cook on low for 4 to 5 hours. Remove chicken from pot. Turn control to high. Dissolve cornstarch in small amount of cold water; stir into sauce. Cook on high for about 15 minutes. Makes 8 chicken rolls. Serve with sauce.

BUSY WOMAN'S ROAST CHICKEN

1 (6-oz.) pkg. stove-top dressing
1 1/4 cups water
1/4 cup sauterne wine

12 carrots, peeled and cut into 2-inch pieces
1 (4 to 5-lb.) roasting chicken
Salt and pepper

Prepare dressing according to package directions with 1 1/4 cups water. Set aside to cool. When cool, stir in sauterne. Meanwhile, in saucepan, cook carrots in small amount of water for 5 minutes. Drain and place in slow-cooking pot. Rinse and dry chicken; stuff with dressing. Place on top of carrots in slow-cooking pot. Sprinkle with salt and pepper. Cover pot and cook on low for 6 to 8 hours or until chicken is tender. If a browner chicken is preferred, place in baking pan in 400° oven for about 15 minutes. Slice chicken; serve with carrots. Makes 6 to 7 servings.

CHICKEN BREASTS, SALTIMBOCCA STYLE

3 whole chicken breasts, skinned and boned
6 small slices ham
6 small slices Swiss cheese
1/4 cup flour
1/4 cup grated Parmesan cheese
1 tsp. salt

1/2 tsp. powdered sage
1/4 tsp. pepper
1/3 cup salad oil
1 (10 1/2-oz.) can condensed cream of chicken
 soup
1/2 cup dry white wine

Cut each boned chicken breast in half; pound until thin between two sheets of waxed paper or foil. Place slice of ham and cheese on each piece of chicken. Roll up and tuck ends in; secure with small skewer or toothpick. Dip chicken rolls into mixture of flour, Parmesan cheese, salt, sage, and pepper. Save any leftover flour mixture. Chill chicken for at least one hour. In large skillet or pot with browning unit, heat oil and saute chicken on all sides. Place browned chicken in slow-cooking pot; add soup mixed with wine. Cover and cook on low for 4 to 5 hours. Turn control to high. Thicken with leftover flour dissolved in a small amount of water. Cook on high for 10 minutes. Serve with hot rice. Makes 6 chicken rolls.

CHICKEN PARMIGIANA

3 whole chicken breasts (or 6 halves)
1 egg
1 tsp. salt
1/4 tsp. pepper
1 cup dry bread crumbs
1/2 cup butter

1 small eggplant, cut into large slices (about
 3/4-inch thick)
1 (10 1/2-oz.) can pizza sauce
6 slices mozzarella cheese
Parmesan cheese

If using whole chicken breasts, cut into halves. In bowl, beat egg, salt, and pepper. Dip chicken into egg. Then coat with crumbs. In large skillet or slow-cooking pot with browning unit, saute chicken in butter. Arrange eggplant and chicken in pot (place eggplant on bottom or it will not cook completely). Pour pizza sauce over chicken. Cover and cook on low 6 to 8 hours. Add mozzarella cheese; sprinkle Parmesan cheese on top. Cover and cook 15 minutes. Makes 6 servings.

CHICKEN NAPOLI

1 frying chicken, cut up
1 tsp. seasoned salt
1/4 cup flour
1/2 tsp. salt
1/8 tsp. pepper

2 tbs. grated Parmesan cheese
1/2 tsp. paprika
1 lb. zucchini, cut into thin slices
1/2 cup chicken bouillon
1 (4-oz.) can mushrooms, drained

Sprinkle chicken with seasoned salt. Combine flour, salt, pepper, cheese, and paprika; coat chicken with mixture. Place zucchini in bottom of slow-cooking pot. Pour bouillon over zucchini. Arrange coated chicken over all. Cover and cook on low for 5 to 6 hours or until tender. Turn control to high. Add mushrooms, cover and cook on high another 10 or 15 minutes. Makes 4 to 6 servings.

CHICKEN TETRAZZINI

1 (2 1/2 to 3-lb.) chicken, cut up
1 cup water
1/2 cup dry white wine
1 medium onion, chopped
1 tsp. salt
1/4 tsp. thyme
1/4 tsp. pepper
2 tbs. minced parsley

1/3 cup butter or margarine
1/3 cup flour
1/2 cup light cream
1 (4-oz.) can mushrooms, drained
8 oz. spaghetti, broken into 2-inch pieces,
   cooked and drained
1/2 cup grated Parmesan cheese

In slow-cooking pot, combine chicken, water, wine, onion, salt, thyme, pepper, and parsley. Cover and cook on low 10 to 12 hours or until chicken is very well done. Remove chicken. Strain broth into bowl or container. Remove meat from bones. Cut chicken into slivers and set aside.* Add butter to slow-cooking pot; turn control to high. Melt butter; stir in flour. Gradually pour in broth, then cream. Cook on high 30 minutes or until bubbly. Stir in cooked chicken, mushrooms, and cooked spaghetti. Cover and cook on high 15 minutes. Sprinkle top with Parmesan cheese. Makes 8 servings.

*Chicken and broth may be cooked the day ahead of serving and refrigerated at this point. Then, one hour before serving time, combine with remaining ingredients and complete.

Chicken Cacciatora Photo: Theodore R. Sills. Courtesy National Macaroni Institute

CHICKEN CACCIATORA

1 (2 1/2 to 3-lb.) broiler-fryer chicken, cut-up
1/4 cup salad oil
1 onion, chopped
2 (8-oz.) cans tomato sauce
1 tsp. dried oregano leaves, crushed
1/4 tsp. dried thyme leaves, crushed

1 tsp. salt
1/4 tsp. pepper
1 clove garlic, minced
2 tbs. dry red wine
1 (2-oz.) can sliced mushrooms, drained
Cooked spaghetti

In large skillet or slow-cooking pot with browning unit, brown chicken in hot oil. Drain. In slow-cooking pot, combine chicken with onion, tomato sauce, oregano, thyme, salt, pepper, garlic and wine. Cover and cook on low for 4 to 5 hours. Stir in drained mushrooms. Spoon over hot cooked spaghetti. Makes 4 to 5 servings.

POACHED CHICKEN

1 stewing chicken (5 to 6 lbs.) or 2 broiler-
   fryers
Water
1 stalk celery, halved (with leaves)
1 carrot, peeled and halved
1 small onion, halved

1 tsp. salt
3 or 4 sprigs parsley
1 small bay leaf
2 whole cloves
1/2 tsp. thyme leaves

Sauce:

4 tbs. butter or margarine
1/4 cup flour
1 cup chicken broth or bouillon
1/2 tsp. salt

1/8 tsp. pepper
1/4 cup chopped parsley
1/2 cup heavy cream
2 tbs. butter or margarine

In slow-cooking pot, cover chicken with water. Add celery, carrot, onion, and salt. Tie parsley, bay leaf, cloves, and thyme in small square of cheesecloth. Add to pot. Cover and cook on low for 7 to 9 hours. Melt 4 tbs. butter in medium saucepan. Stir in flour and cook over low heat several minutes. Gradually stir in broth; simmer until smooth. Add salt, pepper, parsley, and cream. Just before serving, beat in remaining 2 tbs. butter, 1 tbs. at a time. Remove chicken from pot; slice and serve with creamy sauce. Makes 5 to 7 servings.

CHICKEN & HERB DUMPLINGS

1 (2 1/2 to 3-lb.) chicken, cut up
1 tsp. salt
1/4 tsp. pepper
2 whole cloves
8 to 10 small white onions
1 clove garlic, minced
1/4 tsp. powdered marjoram

1/4 tsp. powdered thyme
1 bay leaf
1/2 cup dry white wine
1 cup dairy sour cream
1 cup packaged biscuit mix
1 tbs. chopped parsley
6 tbs. milk

Sprinkle chicken with salt and pepper; place in slow-cooking pot. Insert cloves in one onion. Put all onions in pot. Add garlic, marjoram, thyme, bay leaf, and wine. Cover and cook on low 5 to 6 hours. Remove bay leaf and cloves. Stir in sour cream. Turn control to high. Combine biscuit mix with parsley; stir milk into biscuit mix with fork until well moistened. Drop dumplings from teaspoon around edge of pot. Cover and cook on high for 30 minutes. Makes 5 servings.

ANNE'S CHICKEN

1 frying chicken, cut up
2 tbs. melted butter or margarine
Salt and pepper
2 tbs. dry Italian salad dressing mix

1 (10 3/4-oz.) can condensed mushroom soup,
   undiluted
2 (3-oz.) packages cream cheese, cut into cubes
1/2 cup sauterne or sherry
1 tbs. chopped onion

Wash chicken and pat dry. Brush with butter. Sprinkle with salt and pepper. Place in slow-cooking pot. Sprinkle dry salad mix over. Cover and cook on low for 5 to 6 hours. About 3/4 hour before serving, mix soup, cream cheese, wine, and onion in small saucepan. Cook until smooth. Pour over chicken in pot. Cover and cook 30 minutes on low. Serve with sauce. Makes 4 to 5 servings. Serve with rice or noodles.

BRUNSWICK STEW

1 (2 1/2 to 3-lb.) chicken, cut up
2 qts. water
1 onion, chopped
2 cups cubed cooked ham
3 potatoes, diced
2 (16-oz.) cans tomatoes, cut up
1 (10-oz.) package frozen lima beans, partially thawed

1 (10-oz.) package frozen whole kernel corn, partially thawed
2 tsp. salt
1/2 tsp. seasoned salt
1 tsp. sugar
1/4 tsp. pepper

In slow-cooking pot, combine chicken with water, onion, ham, and potatoes. Cook, covered, on low for 4 to 5 hours or until chicken is done. Lift chicken out of pot. Remove meat from bones. Return chicken meat to pot. Add tomatoes, beans, corn, salt, seasoned salt, sugar, and pepper. Turn control to high. Cover and cook on high 1 hour. Serve in large individual bowls. Makes 8 servings.

BARBECUED TURKEY LEGS

4 uncooked turkey drumsticks*
Salt and pepper
1/4 cup molasses
1/4 cup vinegar

1/4 cup catsup
2 tbs. Worcestershire sauce
1/2 tsp. hickory smoke salt
1 tbs. instant minced onion

Sprinkle turkey with salt and pepper. Place in slow-cooking pot. Combine remaining ingredients; pour over turkey. Cover and cook on low for 5 to 7 hours. If turkey legs are small, serve one thigh or one drumstick per person; if large, slice off cooked meat and serve with sauce. Makes 4 to 6 servings.

*Use 4 thighs, 2 drumsticks and 2 thighs, or 4 drumsticks. Drumsticks may get done first, so check them before thighs. Cooking time on both parts will vary with the size. Use smaller size parts in smaller cooking pot.

STUFFED TURKEY BREAST*

1/4 cup melted butter
1 small onion, finely chopped
1/2 cup finely chopped celery
1 (2 1/2-oz.) package bacon croutons
1 cup chicken bouillon
2 tbs. fresh minced parsley
1/2 tsp. poultry seasoning

1 whole uncooked turkey breast or 2 halves
  (about 5 lbs.)
Salt and pepper
Cheesecloth (about 24 x 36 inches for each
  turkey breast)
Dry white wine

Combine butter, onion, celery, croutons, bouillon, parsley, and poultry seasoning. Cut turkey breast in thick slices, from breastbone to rib cage, leaving slices attached to bone. Sprinkle turkey with salt and pepper. Soak cheesecloth in wine. Set turkey on cheesecloth. Stuff bread mixture into slits of turkey. Fold one end of cheesecloth over other to cover meat. Place on metal rack or trivet in slow-cooking pot. Cover pot and cook on low for 7 to 9 hours or until tender. Pour additional wine over turkey during cooking. Remove from pot and take cheesecloth off immediately. If browner breast is preferred, remove from pot and brown in 400°F. oven for 15 to 20 minutes. Let stand 10 minutes. Drippings may be thickened for gravy if desired. Serve each person one or more thick slices of turkey with dressing in between. Makes 8 or 9 servings.

*This recipe designed for 4 1/2 quart or larger slow-cooking pot.

1/Cut turkey breast in thick slices from breastbone to rib cage, leaving slices attached to bone.
2/Set turkey on cheesecloth. Stuff bread mixture into slits of turkey.
3/Fold one end of cheesecloth over other to cover meat. Place meat on rack or trivet in slow-cooking pot.

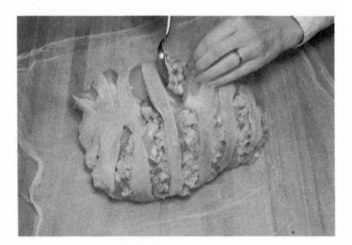

Cran-Orange Turkey Roll   Courtesy National Turkey Federation

CRAN-ORANGE TURKEY ROLL

1/4 cup sugar
2 tbs. cornstarch
3/4 cup orange marmalade
1 cup fresh cranberries, ground or finely
   chopped

1 (2 to 2 1/2-lb.) frozen turkey roll, partially
   thawed
Salt and pepper

In small saucepan, blend sugar and cornstarch; stir in marmalade and cranberries. Cook and stir until mixture is bubbly and slightly thickened. Place partially thawed turkey roll in slow-cooking pot. Sprinkle lightly with salt and pepper. Pour sauce over turkey. Cover and cook on low for 9 to 10 hours. (Insert meat thermometer in turkey roll the last 2 or 3 hours; cover and cook until temperature reaches 185°F.) Slice turkey roll; spoon sauce over. Makes 6 servings.

SWEET & SOUR TURKEY WINGS

4 uncooked turkey wings
3 cups chicken broth or bouillon
1/2 cup finely chopped celery
1 tsp. salt
3 tbs. cornstarch
1/4 cup brown sugar

1/4 cup vinegar
1/4 cup soy sauce
1/3 cup chili sauce*
1/2 green pepper, cut into strips
1 (13 1/2-oz.) can pineapple chunks, drained

Separate wings at joints and discard tips. In slow-cooking pot, combine wings, broth, celery, and salt. Cover and cook on low for 4 to 6 hours or until tender. Drain, saving 1 1/2 cups broth for sauce.** In large skillet, combine cornstarch, brown sugar, 1 1/2 cups broth, vinegar, soy sauce, and chili sauce. Cook and stir until thick and clear. Stir in green pepper and pineapple; simmer for 2 minutes. Add drained, cooked wings. Bring to simmer. Serve over rice. Makes 4 servings.

*Bottled tomato sauce similar to catsup.
**Wings may be cooked ahead and refrigerated with broth at this point; sweet-sour sauce may be made just before serving.

Lime-Glazed Cornish Hens   Courtesy Cling Peach Advisory Board

TURKEY LOAF

2 lbs. ground uncooked turkey
1 1/2 cups soft bread crumbs
2 eggs, slightly beaten
1 small onion, minced
1 tsp. prepared horseradish

1 tsp. salt
1 tsp. dry mustard
1/4 cup catsup
1/4 cup evaporated milk

Combine turkey with remaining ingredients. Form into a 7-inch round loaf. Place in bottom of slow-cooking pot. Cover and cook on low for 5 to 6 hours. Makes 6 to 7 servings. Good served hot with cranberry sauce or sliced cold for sandwiches.

RED RAISIN CORNISH HENS

1 (6-oz.) package stove-top stuffing mix
4 to 5 Cornish hens

Salt and pepper

Sauce:
1 (10-oz.) jar red currant jelly
1/2 cup golden raisins
1/4 cup butter or margarine

2 tsp. lemon juice
1/4 tsp. allspice

Mix stuffing according to package directions and stuff hens. Sprinkle with salt and pepper. Place trivet in slow-cooking pot. For 3 1/2 quart pot, place hens on end, neck end down. In saucepan, combine jelly, raisins, butter, lemon juice and allspice. Cook on low heat, stirring constantly, until blended. Brush some of the sauce on hens in the pot. (Brush hens once during cooking, if possible.) Cover slow-cooking pot and cook on low for 5 to 7 hours. Spoon remaining sauce over hens at serving time. Makes 4 to 5 servings.

LIME-GLAZED CORNISH HENS

4 to 5 Cornish game hens
1 (8-oz.) package stuffing mix
1/4 cup melted butter
2 tbs. brown sugar

2 tbs. lime juice
2 tbs. dry white wine
2 tsp. soy sauce

Thaw hens, if frozen. Follow directions on package for stuffing mix. Spoon stuffing into cavity of each hen. Mix butter with sugar, lime juice, wine, and soy sauce. Brush hens with sauce. Place trivet in slow-cooking pot. For 3 1/2 quart pot, place hens on end, neck end down. Cover and cook on low for 5 to 7 hours. Brush with sauce once during cooking if possible. Makes 4 to 5 servings.

BURGUNDY-BASTED DUCKLING

1 (4 to 5-lb.) ready-to-cook duckling*
1/4 cup Burgundy wine
1/4 cup lemon juice
1 tbs. melted butter or margarine
1 tbs. Worcestershire sauce

1 clove garlic, minced
1 tsp. salt
1 tsp. dried marjoram, crushed
1/4 tsp. pepper
2 or 3 drops bottled hot pepper sauce

With a fork, prick skin of duckling all over at approximately two-inch intervals. Place metal rack or trivet in bottom of slow-cooking pot. Set duckling, breast side up, in pot. Combine Burgundy, lemon juice, butter, Worcestershire sauce, garlic, salt, marjoram, pepper, and pepper sauce. Brush about half the sauce over duckling. Cover and cook on low for 7 to 9 hours. If possible, remove excess fat, brush duckling with more sauce, and turn duckling once during cooking. Remove excess fat again at end of cooking time on low. Then turn control to high, brush with remaining sauce and cook a final 30 minutes. If a browner bird is desired, it may be placed on a broiler pan or heat-proof platter and browned in 400°F. oven for about 15 or 20 minutes. Makes 4 servings.

*If desired, duckling may be cut into halves or quarters before cooking to fit into 3 1/2 quart or smaller cooking pot.

GOLDEN WEST DUCKLING

1 (4 to 5-lb.) ready-to-cook duckling*
1 (29-oz.) can sliced cling peaches
1 tbs. grated orange peel
1/2 cup dry white wine
2 tbs. honey

1 tbs. soy sauce
1/4 tsp. seasoned salt
1 tbs. cornstarch
1 tbs. cold water

Cut or have butcher cut duckling into halves, lengthwise.* Prick skin with fork at about 2-inch intervals. Place on trivet in slow-cooking pot, cut side down. Drain peaches, saving syrup. Combine 1 cup peach syrup with orange peel, wine, honey, soy sauce and seasoned salt. Brush some of the sauce over duckling. Cover and cook on low for 7 to 9 hours or until tender. (If possible, drain excess fat and brush with sauce once or twice while cooking.) Dissolve cornstarch in water. Stir into remaining sauce. Cook sauce in small saucepan until slightly thickened. Add drained peaches to sauce, heat and serve with duckling. Serve duckling with bananas and cooked rice. Makes 4 servings.

*If your slow-cooking pot is 3 1/2 quarts or smaller, cut duckling into quarters so it will fit into pot.

IMPERIAL DUCKLING

1 ready-to-cook duckling (4 to 5 lbs.)*
2 tbs. minced onion
1/4 tsp. tarragon leaves
2 tbs. butter or margarine
1/2 cup orange juice
1/8 tsp. salt

1/8 tsp. dry mustard
1/4 cup currant jelly
2 tbs. grated orange peel
2 tbs. port wine
1 orange, peeled and sectioned
1 1/2 tsp. cornstarch

With a fork, prick skin of duckling all over at approximately two-inch intervals. Place duckling, breast side up, on metal rack or trivet in slow-cooking pot. In saucepan, saute onion and tarragon leaves in butter. Add orange juice, salt, mustard, currant jelly, and orange peel. Cook over medium heat, stirring constantly, until jelly is melted. Reduce heat; stir in wine and orange sections. Brush 1/3 of the sauce over duck; cover slow-cooking pot and cook on low 7 to 9 hours. During cooking drain fat and turn duck once, if possible. Stir remaining sauce into cornstarch and cook over medium heat until sauce thickens, then simmer 1 minute. Pour sauce over duck just before serving. Makes 4 servings.

*Duckling may be cut into halves or quarters to fit into 3 1/2 quart or smaller slow-cooking pot.

VEGETABLES

One of the greatest advantages of cooking vegetables in a slow cooker is being able to cook them ahead of time. It is not necessary to watch, stir, or worry about boil overs. You can be doing something else around the house or running errands at the local shopping center. When you return, the vegetables are done. Serve them for dinner or combine with other ingredients in a casserole and brown them in the oven to serve later.

Rules for cooking vegetables vary almost as much as the vegetables themselves. For example, you will discover countless ways to prepare the squash family in your slow cooker. You can stuff acorn squash, glaze banana squash, mash banana squash, and simmer zucchini. You can cook squash in your pot, add other ingredients and finish the dish in the oven.

Carrots, celery, turnips, parsnips and beets take an extra long time to cook in a slow-cooking pot. Strangely enough, *these vegetables take as long or longer to cook than many meats.* Be sure to consider this when combining vegetables with meat.

Recipes for sweet potatoes or yams may be interchanged. Use the one you prefer or whichever is available in your market.

Sweet and white potatoes are delicious when "baked" in a slow-cooking pot. Wash the potatoes but do not actually dry. While still damp, place in slow cooker and cook on low until soft and tender. You cannot use this baking method with all slow cookers. The Use and Care chapter tells which brands you can bake in.

It is wise to turn the control to HIGH when you are cooking most vegetables in a slow cooker. Many of them have a tendency to dry out and discolor when left on LOW for a long time.

RHINELAND SWEET-SOUR RED CABBAGE

4 slices bacon, diced
1/4 cup brown sugar
2 tbs. flour
1 tsp. salt
1/8 tsp. pepper

1/2 cup water
1/4 cup vinegar
1 medium head red cabbage, shredded (6 to
   8 cups)
1 small onion, finely chopped

Cook bacon in skillet or slow-cooking pot with browning unit. Set bacon aside. Combine 1 tbs. of bacon drippings in slow-cooking pot with sugar, flour, salt, and pepper. Stir in water and vinegar; add cabbage and onion. Cover and cook on low 3 to 4 hours. Spoon into serving bowl; sprinkle cooked bacon on top. Makes 6 to 8 servings.

MOTHER-IN-LAW'S SAUERKRAUT

4 slices bacon, diced
1 (1-lb. 11-oz.) can sauerkraut
1 head cabbage, chopped
1 large onion, diced

1 tbs. butter or margarine
1 tsp. sugar
1/2 tsp. salt
1/8 tsp. pepper

In small skillet, cook bacon, saving drippings. In slow-cooking pot, combine sauerkraut, cabbage, onion, butter, sugar, salt, and pepper. Pour cooked bacon and drippings over all. Cover and cook on low for 3 to 5 hours. Makes 8 servings.

ORANGE-GLAZED CARROTS

3 cups thinly sliced carrots
2 cups water
1/4 tsp. salt

3 tbs. butter or margarine
3 tbs. orange marmalade
2 tbs. chopped pecans

Combine carrots, water, and salt in slow-cooking pot. Cover and cook on high 2 to 3 hours or until carrots are done. Drain well; stir in remaining ingredients. Cover and cook on high 20 to 30 minutes. Makes 5 to 6 servings.

CARROTS IN DILLED WINE SAUCE

8 medium carrots, cut into small sticks
1/2 cup chicken bouillon
1/2 cup dry white wine
1/2 tsp. dried dill weed
2 tsp. instant minced onion

1/4 tsp. garlic salt
1 tbs. lemon juice
2 tbs. cornstarch
2 tbs. cold water

Place carrots in slow-cooking pot. Combine bouillon, wine, dill, onion, garlic salt, and lemon juice. Pour over carrots. Cover and cook on high 2 to 3 hours. Dissolve cornstarch in water. Stir into carrot mixture. Cook on high 10 minutes or until slightly thickened. Makes 6 servings.

CORN PUDDING

3 slightly beaten eggs
2 cups cooked or canned whole kernel corn, drained
2 cups milk, scalded

1 tbs. instant minced onion
1 tbs. melted butter
1 tsp. sugar
1 tsp. salt

Combine ingredients; pour into greased 1 1/2-qt. baking dish.* Cover with foil or lid (do not use plastic). Set metal rack or trivet in bottom of slow-cooking pot. Pour 4 cups hot water in pot. Set baking dish on rack in hot water. Cover pot and cook on high for 2 to 2 1/2 hours or until done. Makes 6 servings.

*1 1/2-qt. baking dish fits into 4 1/2 quart or larger slow-cooking pot.

CORN STUFFING BALLS

1/2 cup celery with leaves, chopped
1 small onion, chopped
1 (17-oz.) can cream-style corn
1/4 cup water
1/8 tsp. pepper

1 tsp. poultry seasoning
1 (8-oz.) package herb-seasoned stuffing mix
2 slightly beaten eggs
1/4 cup melted butter or margarine

In mixing bowl, combine celery, onion, corn, water, pepper, poultry seasoning, stuffing mix, and eggs. Shape into 7 or 8 balls. Place in slow-cooking pot. Pour butter over. Cover and cook on low for 3 to 4 hours. Serve with broiled meats or roasts, or use as extra dressing with turkey.

TAMALE PUFF*

1 (1-lb.) can cream style corn
1 (1-lb.) can whole kernel corn, drained
1 (4-oz.) can chopped green chilies, drained
1 small onion, finely chopped

4 eggs
1 (16-oz.) can tamales
1/2 cup grated cheddar cheese

In medium mixing bowl, combine cream style and whole kernel corn, chilies and onion. In small bowl, beat eggs until frothy; fold into corn mixture. Spoon corn-egg mixture into 2 1/2-qt. baking dish. Cut tamales in half; arrange on top. Sprinkle with cheese. Cover baking dish with foil. Place metal rack or trivet in bottom of slow-cooking pot. Pour 2 cups hot water in pot. Set filled baking dish on trivet in pot. Cover pot and cook on high for 2 1/2 to 3 1/2 hours. Makes 6 servings.

*This recipe is designed for a 4 1/2 quart or larger slow-cooking pot.

GREEN BEANS PORTUGUESE STYLE

1/4 lb. salt pork
2 lbs. fresh green beans
2 medium tomatoes
2 cups beef bouillon

1/2 tsp. salt
1/2 tsp. sugar
1/4 tsp. pepper

Dice salt pork and spread over bottom of slow-cooking pot. Wash beans. Break each bean into 2 or 3 pieces; place in pot over salt pork. Peel, seed and cube tomatoes; spoon over beans. Add bouillon with salt, sugar, and pepper. Cover and cook on high for 3 to 4 hours or until beans are tender. Drain and serve hot. Makes 8 servings.

TURNIP WHIP

4 turnips, peeled and quartered
4 potatoes, peeled and quartered
2 tbs. minced onion
1 tsp. salt
Water

1/4 cup light cream
2 tbs. soft butter or margarine
1/2 tsp. salt
1/8 tsp. pepper

In slow-cooking pot, combine turnips, potatoes, onion and 1 tsp. salt. Cover with water. Cover pot and cook on low for 6 to 8 hours or until vegetables are tender. Drain well. Mash; add cream, butter, 1/2 tsp. salt and pepper. Beat until fluffy. Makes 6 servings.

ORANGE-GLAZED PARSNIPS

8 to 10 medium parsnips
Water
1 tsp. salt
2 tbs. butter or margarine

2 tbs. honey
1/2 tsp. seasoned salt
1/4 cup orange juice
1/2 tsp. grated orange peel

Wash and peel parsnips. Cut into sticks about 1/4-inch thick. Cover with water in slow-cooking pot; add salt. Cover and cook on high for 2 to 4 hours or until tender. Drain. Meanwhile, in saucepan, melt butter, stir in honey, seasoned salt, orange juice, and peel. Heat to boiling. Pour over drained parsnips. Makes 5 to 6 servings.

STUFFED POTATOES

5 to 6 large baking potatoes
3 tbs. butter
1/2 cup milk
1/2 cup dairy sour cream

1 tsp. salt
1/8 tsp. pepper
2 tbs. grated Parmesan cheese
Chopped chives

Wash potatoes; drain but do not dry. Place damp potatoes in slow-cooking pot. Cover pot and cook on low for 6 to 8 hours or until tender. Remove from pot. Cut a thick, lengthwise slice from top of each potato. Scoop hot potato pulp into mixing bowl, saving the potato "shell." Add butter, milk, sour cream, salt, and pepper. Beat until fluffy, adding more milk if necessary. Spoon mixture into shells, mounding tops. Sprinkle with cheese. Place in shallow baking pan. Bake in 425°F. oven for 15 minutes or until hot and lightly browned. Top with chopped chives. Makes 5 to 6 servings.

PEACH CHUTNEY

4 cups diced peaches (two 29-oz. cans)
1 cup raisins
1 small onion, chopped
1 clove garlic, minced
1 tbs. mustard seed

1 tsp. chopped dried red chilies
1/4 cup chopped crystallized ginger
1 tsp. salt
3/4 cup vinegar
1/2 cup brown sugar

Combine ingredients in slow-cooking pot. Cover and cook on low 4 to 6 hours. Remove lid; turn control to high and cook for 1 or 2 hours. Makes about 4 cups. Serve with curried lamb, shrimp or chicken.

ACORN SQUASH, INDONESIAN

3 acorn squash
Salt and pepper
1/4 cup melted butter

1/3 cup chutney*
1/3 cup flake coconut

Cut squash in half; remove seeds. Wash and drain excess water but do not dry. Sprinkle with salt and pepper. Place in slow-cooking pot. Cover and cook on low for 3 to 5 hours or until tender. Remove from pot; set, cut side up, on broiler pan or heat-proof platter. Brush inside of squash with butter. Mix chutney and coconut; spoon into cavity of squash. Bake in 400°F. oven for about 15 minutes or until bubbly. Makes 6 servings.

*Make chutney in slow-cooking pot (see recipe on previous page).

CANDIED BANANA SQUASH*

6 serving-size pieces banana squash
1/4 cup granulated sugar
1/4 cup packed brown sugar

1/4 cup melted butter
1/4 tsp. salt

Remove seeds and membrane from squash. Arrange squash, skin side down, in slow-cooking pot. Cover and cook on low for 5 to 6 hours or until almost done. Combine sugars with butter and salt. Turn control to high. Spoon sauce over squash. Cover and cook on high for 15 to 20 minutes. Makes 6 servings.

*This recipe is designed for a 4 1/2 quart or larger slow-cooking pot.

STUFFED BUTTERNUT SQUASH

3 butternut squash
1 cup hot water
3 tbs. soft butter
1/4 tsp. salt
1 tbs. corn syrup

2 tbs. raisins
1/4 cup chopped walnuts
1/4 cup brown sugar
2 tbs. melted butter

Cut squash in half; remove seeds. Place metal rack or trivet in bottom of slow-cooking pot. Pour in 1 cup hot water. Arrange squash on rack. Cover pot and cook on high 2 to 3 hours or until done. Remove from pot; scrape out pulp down to the skin. Add 3 tbs. butter, salt, and corn syrup to pulp and beat until smooth. Stir in raisins and nuts. Put filling back into shells; place on broiler pan. Combine brown sugar with 2 tbs. melted butter. Drizzle over top of filled squash. Place under broiler several minutes or until top is slightly crusty. Makes 6 servings.

STUFFED PATTYPAN SQUASH

8 to 10 pattypan squash (light green summer
   squash)
Water

1 tsp. salt
1 (10-oz.) package frozen creamed peas or mixed
   creamed vegetables

In slow-cooking pot, cover squash with water; add salt. Cover and cook on low for 6 to 7 hours or until squash is tender. Drain. Meanwhile, cook peas or vegetables according to package directions. Scoop out squash pulp in center. Fill with hot creamed peas or hot mixed creamed vegetables. Makes 5 to 6 servings.

HERBED SQUASH AU GRATIN

8 to 10 summer squash (about 2 lbs.)
Water
1 tsp. salt

1/4 cup butter or margarine
2 cups herb-seasoned croutons
1/2 cup grated cheddar cheese

Cut squash into 1/4-inch thick crosswise slices. Cover with water in slow-cooking pot. Add salt. Cover and cook on low for 3 to 4 hours or until tender. Drain. Meanwhile, melt butter in small skillet. Stir in croutons; heat until lightly browned. Add cheese. Sprinkle over well-drained squash. Makes 6 to 8 servings.

SQUASH MEDLEY

8 unpeeled summer squash (about 1 lb.)
1/2 tsp. salt
2 small tomatoes, peeled and chopped
1/2 small green pepper, chopped

1/4 cup sliced green onions
1 cup chicken bouillon
4 slices bacon, cooked and crumbled
1/4 cup fine dry bread crumbs

Thinly slice squash; sprinkle with salt. In slow-cooking pot, arrange alternate layers of squash with tomatoes, green pepper, and onions. Pour bouillon over. Top with bacon, then bread crumbs. Cover pot and cook on low for 4 to 6 hours. Makes 5 to 6 servings.

DOUBLE SQUASH COMBO

1 1/2 lbs. zucchini
1 1/2 lbs. summer squash
1/2 tsp. salt
1/4 tsp. pepper

1/8 tsp. garlic salt
1/4 cup butter or margarine
3 tbs. fine dry bread crumbs
3 tbs. grated Parmesan cheese

Cut both kinds of squash into 1/2-inch pieces. Put in bottom of slow-cooking pot. Sprinkle with salt, pepper, and garlic salt. Dot with butter; sprinkle with crumbs and cheese. Cover and cook on low for 6 to 7 hours or until tender. Makes 6 to 8 servings.

YAM PUDDING

6 large yams or sweet potatoes
1/4 cup butter or margarine
1/4 cup brown sugar
2 tsp. grated lemon peel

1 tbs. lemon juice
1/2 tsp. salt
1/3 cup brown sugar
1/2 cup slivered almonds

Wash yams; drain but do not dry. Set in slow-cooking pot. Cover and cook on low for 4 to 6 hours (depending on size and shape). Cool, peel and place in large bowl. Mash until smooth. Add butter, 1/4 cup brown sugar, lemon peel, juice and salt; mix well. Spoon into greased 1 1/2-qt. baking dish. Sprinkle remaining 1/3 cup brown sugar and almonds on top. Bake in 350°F. oven for 40 to 50 minutes. Makes 6 to 8 servings. This recipe not suitable for Cornwall or Sears tray-type Crockery Cookers.

CANDIED YAMS & CRANBERRIES

6 medium yams or sweet potatoes
1/2 cup butter or margarine
3/4 cup light brown sugar (lightly packed)

2 cups fresh cranberries
1 tsp. salt
1/8 tsp. pepper

Wash yams or potatoes; drain but do not dry. Set in slow-cooking pot. Cover and cook on low for 4 to 6 hours (depending on size and shape). Peel and cut into quarters. Place in 2-quart casserole. In medium saucepan, melt butter; add sugar, cranberries, salt and pepper. Cook, stirring constantly, over medium heat until cranberries pop and sugar dissolves. Pour over yams in casserole.* Cover and bake in 350°F. oven for 30 minutes. Makes 6 servings. This recipe not suitable for Cornwall or Sears tray-type Crockery Cookers.

*Casserole may be refrigerated and baked later. If cold, add 10 to 15 minutes to oven time.

SAUSAGE-STUFFED YAMS

6 medium yams or sweet potatoes
2 tbs. butter or margarine, melted
2 tbs. milk
1 egg

1 tsp. salt
1/4 tsp. dried oregano leaves
4 ozs. smoky link sausage

Wash yams; drain but do not dry. Set in slow-cooking pot. Cover and cook on low for 4 to 6 hours (depending on size and shape). Cut tops from yams; carefully scoop out centers and mash in large bowl. Add butter, milk, egg, salt, and oregano; beat until smooth. Add sausage; mix well. Pile into yam shells. Bake in 400°F. oven for 15 to 20 minutes. Makes 6 servings. This recipe is not suitable for Cornwall or Sears tray-type Crockery Cookers.

Sausage-Stuffed Yams, Candied Yams and Cranberries, Yam Pudding
Courtesy United Fresh Fruit and Vegetable Association

CREOLE ZUCCHINI

2 lbs. zucchini
1 small green pepper, chopped
1 small onion, chopped
1 clove garlic, minced
1 tsp. salt

1/4 tsp. pepper
4 tomatoes, peeled and chopped
2 tbs. butter or margarine
2 tbs. minced parsley

Cut zucchini into 1/4-inch slices. In slow-cooking pot, combine zucchini with green pepper, onion, garlic, salt, and pepper. Top with chopped tomatoes, then butter. Cover and cook on high for about 2 hours or until tender. Sprinkle with chopped parsley. Makes 6 to 7 servings. This recipe is not suitable for Cornwall or Sears tray-type Crockery Cookers.

STUFFED HONEYED SWEET POTATOES

5 to 6 sweet potatoes
1/2 cup soft butter
1/4 cup light cream
2 tbs. honey

2 tbs. dark rum
1/2 tsp. cardamom
1/4 tsp. salt
2 tbs. chopped walnuts

Wash potatoes; drain excess water. Place damp potatoes in slow-cooking pot. Cover and cook on low 5 to 6 hours or until done.* Cut off the top third of each potato lengthwise and scoop out, leaving a 1/4-inch shell. Mash potato pulp with butter, cream, honey, rum, cardamom, and salt. Return mixture to shell. Top with walnuts. Arrange on shallow baking sheet. Bake in 425°F. oven for 15 minutes. Makes 5 to 6 servings. This recipe is not suitable for Cornwall or Sears tray-type Crockery Cookers.

*If desired, potatoes may be refrigerated at this point, then scooped out and filled just before serving. Add about 5 or 10 minutes to baking time if potatoes are cold.

SLOW COOKERY SWEET POTATOES

5 medium sweet potatoes or yams

Wash potatoes. Drain but do not dry. Set in slow-cooking pot. Cover and cook on low for 4 to 6 hours (depending on size and shape of potatoes). Split tops and serve hot with butter. For a sweet potato casserole, let potatoes cool; then peel and slice. This recipe is not suitable for Cornwall or Sears tray-type Crockery Cookers.

Zucchini Casserole   Courtesy Western Grower's Association

ZUCCHINI CASSEROLE

1 lb. lean ground beef
1 medium onion, chopped
3 (8-oz.) cans tomato sauce
1/2 cup dry red wine
1/4 tsp. oregano
1/8 tsp. garlic salt

1/4 tsp. basil
1/2 tsp. salt
1/8 tsp. seasoned pepper
4 to 5 zucchini
1/4 cup grated Parmesan cheese

In large skillet or slow-cooking pot with browning unit, cook beef and onion until meat loses its red color. Pour off excess fat. In slow-cooking pot, combine beef and onion with tomato sauce, wine, oregano, garlic salt, basil, salt, and pepper. Cover and cook on low for 4 to 5 hours.* Pour into greased shallow baking dish. In the meantime, cook whole zucchini in a regular pan of boiling salted water about 15 minutes or until barely tender. Cut lengthwise in halves and arrange, cut side up, on top of meat mixture in baking dish. Sprinkle with cheese. Bake in 350°F. oven 30 to 45 minutes. Makes 5 to 6 servings.

*May be refrigerated at this point and assembled the next day if desired. Bake an additional 5 to 10 minutes if you refrigerate it.

MIXED VEGETABLES EN POT

2 (10-oz.) packages frozen mixed vegetables,
   partially thawed
1/2 cup finely chopped celery
2 (10 3/4-oz.) cans condensed cream of
   celery soup

1/2 tsp. seasoned salt
1 packet (about 1/2 oz.) toasted onion dip mix
1/2 cup water
2 tbs. melted butter or margarine

In slow-cooking pot, combine mixed vegetables with celery. In medium bowl, mix soup with seasoned salt, dry dip mix, water, and melted butter. Pour over vegetables in pot. Cover and cook on low for 4 to 5 hours or until vegetables are tender. Makes 6 servings.

STEWED TOMATOES

4 or 5 large ripe tomatoes
2 tbs. butter or margarine
1 medium onion, thinly sliced
1/2 cup chopped celery
1/4 cup chopped green pepper
1/2 tsp. sugar

1/2 tsp. dried sweet basil
1 small bay leaf
1 tsp. salt
1/8 tsp. pepper
2 tbs. chopped parsley

Quickly dip tomatoes in boiling water; remove skin. Quarter tomatoes; remove core and seeds. In slow-cooking pot, combine all ingredients except parsley. Cover and cook on low for 8 to 9 hours. Remove bay leaf. Sprinkle top with parsley. Makes 4 to 5 servings.

APPETIZERS
&
BEVERAGES

You will have more time with your guests when you serve hot beverages or appetizers in a slow cooker.

Several hours before a party, combine the ingredients for one of the hot drinks. Turn the control on the slow cooker to LOW and the drink will be ready to serve when your guests arrive. What's more, it will be kept hot in a slow cooker without fear of scorching, boiling over or sticking to the pan. Each person can serve himself whenever he is ready for a cup of cheer. This is an especially good way to plan a get-together after the theater or ball game. You can plug in the slow cooker with ingredients for a hot drink, leave for the show, and return with your friends and immediately offer them a hot drink.

Exact times are relatively unimportant when brewing most hot punches. After several hours, the various fruit juices blend together for a smooth taste. However, if left on too many hours over the suggested time, they may become slightly bitter.

Hot appetizers stay hot in a slow cooker. There is no reason for you to rush back and forth to the range to serve hot snacks. Just heat them in a slow cooker. Guests can help themselves whenever they are ready for another hot snack.

If you heat cheese or bean dip in a slow cooker, it will be the right consistency and temperature for all to enjoy.

You take it easy by letting your pot keep your favorite appetizer hot at your next party. Relax! *Enjoy* the festivities.

ZIPPY TOMATO APPETIZER

1 (10 1/2-oz.) can condensed beef broth
1/2 tsp. dried marjoram, crushed

1 (46-oz.) can vegetable juice cocktail
1 tbs. lemon juice

In slow-cooking pot, combine broth, marjoram, vegetable juice cocktail, and lemon juice. Cover and heat on low for 2 to 3 hours. Serve hot from slow-cooking pot. Makes 8 to 10 servings.

HOME-STYLE TOMATO JUICE

10 to 12 large tomatoes
1 tsp. salt
1 tsp. seasoned salt

1/4 tsp. pepper
1 tbs. sugar

Wash and drain tomatoes. Remove core and blossom ends. Place in slow-cooking pot. Cover and cook on low 4 to 6 hours or until tomatoes are done. Press through sieve or food mill. Add seasonings; chill. Makes about 4 cups juice.

SPICY TOMATO JUICE COCKTAIL

4 lbs. fresh tomatoes (12 to 14)
1/2 cup chopped celery
1/4 cup chopped onion
2 tbs. lemon juice
1 1/2 tsp. sugar

1 tsp. salt
1 tsp. prepared horseradish
1 tsp. Worcestershire sauce
1/8 tsp. bottled hot pepper sauce

Wash tomatoes; remove stem ends and cores. Chop tomatoes. In slow-cooking pot, combine tomatoes, celery, and onions. Cover and cook on low for 8 to 10 hours. Press through food mill or sieve. Return juice to pot. Cook on high for 30 minutes. Add lemon juice, sugar, salt, horseradish, Worcestershire sauce, and hot sauce. Cook on high for another 10 minutes. Chill. Makes about 6 cups.

APPETIZER RIBS

3 to 4 lbs. spareribs. cut into individual ribs*
Salt and pepper
2 cups water

Garlic salt
1 (8-oz.) bottle Russian salad dressing
1 (6-oz.) can pineapple juice

Sprinkle ribs with salt and pepper. Place in slow-cooking pot; pour water over them. Cover and cook on low for 6 to 7 hours or until tender. Drain. Arrange ribs on broiler pan; sprinkle with garlic salt. Make sauce by combining salad dressing and pineapple juice. Brush ribs with half the sauce. Broil until brown; turn, brush other side and brown. Makes 8 to 10 appetizer servings.

*If possible, ask the butcher to cut each rib in half, crosswise, so they will be a more convenient size to handle as an appetizer.

FINGER DRUMSTICKS

1 1/2 pounds chicken wings (12 to 15)
Salt and pepper
1 cup chicken bouillon
1 tbs. cornstarch
1/4 cup sugar
1/2 tsp. salt

1/4 tsp. ground ginger
1/8 tsp. pepper
3 tbs. lemon juice
2 tbs. soy sauce
1/8 tsp. garlic salt

Cut off and discard wing tips; divide each wing in half by cutting through joint with a sharp knife. Sprinkle wings with salt and pepper. Place in slow-cooking pot. Pour bouillon over chicken. Cover and cook on low for 4 to 5 hours or until tender. Drain; place on broiler pan. Meanwhile, in small saucepan, combine cornstarch with sugar, salt, ginger, pepper, lemon juice, soy sauce and garlic salt. Simmer, stirring constantly, until mixture thickens. Brush some sauce on chicken; brown under broiler. Turn; brush sauce on chicken and brown other side. Makes about 25 to 30 appetizers. Recipe may be doubled for a party. Keep appetizers hot and serve from slow-cooking pot.

CURRIED ALMONDS

2 tbs. melted butter
1 tbs. curry powder

1/2 tsp. seasoned salt
1 lb. blanched almonds

Combine butter with curry and seasoned salt. Pour over almonds in slow-cooking pot and mix to coat well. Cover and cook on low for 2 to 3 hours. Turn to high. Uncover pot and cook for 1 to 1 1/2 hours. Serve hot or cold, as a snack.

CHILI NUTS

1/4 cup soft or melted butter
2 (12-oz.) cans cocktail peanuts

1 (1 5/8-oz.) package chili seasoning mix

In slow-cooking pot, pour butter over nuts; sprinkle in dry chili mix. Toss together. Cover pot and heat on low for 2 to 2 1/2 hours. Turn control to high. Remove top and cook on high for 10 or 15 minutes. Serve warm or cool in small nut dishes. Makes about 5 cups.

ALL-AMERICAN SNACK

3 cups thin pretzel sticks
4 cups Wheat Chex
4 cups Cheerios
1 (13-oz.) can salted peanuts
1 tsp. garlic salt

1 tsp. celery salt
1/2 tsp. seasoned salt
2 tbs. grated Parmesan cheese
1/4 cup melted butter

In large mixing bowl or slow-cooking pot, mix together pretzels, cereals, and peanuts. Sprinkle with garlic salt, celery salt, seasoned salt, and cheese. Pour melted butter over all; toss until well mixed. Cover and cook in slow-cooking pot on low 3 to 4 hours. Uncover the last 30 to 40 minutes. Serve as appetizer or snack. Makes about 3 quarts.

EAST INDIAN SNACK

1 (5-oz.) can crisp Chinese noodles
1 (6 1/4-oz.) package salted cashew nuts
2 cups Rice Chex
1/2 cup toasted coconut

1 tsp. curry powder
1/4 tsp. ground ginger
1/4 cup melted butter
1 tbs. soy sauce

In mixing bowl or slow-cooking pot, mix together noodles, cashews, Rice Chex, and coconut. Sprinkle with curry and ginger. Add butter and soy sauce. Toss until well mixed. Cover and cook in slow-cooking pot on low 3 to 4 hours. Uncover the last 30 to 40 minutes. Serve as appetizer or snack. Makes about 6 cups.

LIVER PATE BON APPETIT

1 lb. chicken livers
1/2 cup dry wine
1 tsp. instant chicken bouillon or 1 bouillon
  cube
1 tsp. minced parsley
1 tbs. instant minced onion

1/4 tsp. ginger
1/2 tsp. seasoned salt
1 tbs. soy sauce
1/4 tsp. dry mustard
1/4 cup soft butter
1 tbs. brandy

Combine chicken livers in slow-cooking pot with wine, bouillon, parsley, onion, ginger, seasoned salt, soy sauce, and mustard. Cover and cook on low 4 to 5 hours. Let stand in liquid until cool. Drain and place in blender or food grinder. Add butter and brandy. Blend or mix until smooth. Serve with crackers or toast. Makes about 1 1/2 cups.

SHORT-CUT FONDUE DIP

2 (10 3/4-oz.) cans condensed cheese soup
2 cups (1/2 lb.) grated sharp cheddar cheese
1 tbs. Worcestershire sauce
1 tsp. lemon juice

1 (.01-oz.) packet freeze-dried chopped chives
Celery sticks
Cauliflower, cut into flowerets (uncooked)
Corn chips (optional)

Combine condensed soup, grated cheese, Worcestershire sauce, lemon juice, and chives. Cover and heat on low in slow-cooking pot for 2 to 2 1/2 hours. Stir until smooth and well blended. Keep hot in the pot. Dip celery sticks, cauliflower, and corn chips into cheese mixture. Makes 8 to 10 servings.

REFRIED BEAN DIP

1 (20-oz.) can refried beans
1 cup shredded cheddar cheese
1/2 cup chopped green onions

1/4 tsp. salt
2 tbs. bottled taco sauce
Tortilla chips

In slow-cooking pot, combine beans with cheese, onions, salt, and taco sauce. Cover and cook on low for 2 to 2 1/2 hours. Serve hot from the pot. Dip tortilla chips into mixture.

CHILI CON QUESO

1 lb. pasteurized process cheese spread
1 (1-lb.) can chili without beans

4 green onions, chopped
1 (4-oz.) can chopped green chili peppers

Mix all ingredients in slow-cooking pot. Cover and cook on low 2 to 3 hours. Serve hot from the pot. Use as dip for corn chips. Makes about 4 cups.

Chili Con Queso   Courtesy Western Growers Association

HOT SPICED CLARET

2 tbs. sugar
2 tbs. lemon juice
1/2 tsp. ground cinnamon

1/4 tsp. ground nutmeg
1/2 cup hot water
1 (4/5-qt.) bottle claret wine

In slow-cooking pot, combine sugar, lemon juice, cinnamon, nutmeg, and water. Stir until well blended. Pour in wine. Cover pot; heat on low 2 to 2 1/2 hours. Serve hot from the pot. Makes 6 to 8 servings.

WINTER WARM-UP

1 (4/5-qt.) bottle sherry or muscatel
6 cups orange juice

1 tsp. ground cardamom

In slow-cooking pot, combine wine with orange juice and cardamom. Cover and heat on low for 2 to 3 hours. Ladle into heat-proof glasses or mugs. Makes 10 to 12 servings.

TROPICAL TEA WARMER

6 cups boiling water
6 tea bags
1/3 cup sugar
2 tbs. honey

1 1/2 cups orange juice
1 1/2 cups pineapple juice
1 orange, sliced (unpeeled)

Pour boiling water over tea bags in slow-cooking pot.* Cover and let stand 5 minutes. Remove tea bags. Stir in sugar, honey, orange juice, pineapple juice, and orange slices. Cover and heat on low for 2 to 3 hours; serve from pot. Makes 10 servings.

*If slow-cooking pot is cold, warm first with hot tap water.

MEDITERRANEAN COFFEE

2 qts. strong hot coffee
1/4 cup chocolate syrup
1/3 cup sugar
4 cinnamon sticks
1 1/2 tsp. whole cloves

1/2 tsp. anise flavoring
Peel of 1 orange, in strips for twists
Peel of 1 lemon, in strips for twists
Whipped cream

Combine coffee, chocolate syrup, sugar, cinnamon sticks, cloves, and anise in slow-cooking pot. Cover and cook on low for 2 to 3 hours. Serve in cups with twist of lemon, twist of orange, and cap of whipped cream in each. Makes 12 servings.

HOT BUTTERED PUNCH

3/4 cup brown sugar
4 cups water
1/4 tsp. salt
1/4 tsp. nutmeg
1/2 tsp. cinnamon
1/2 tsp. allspice

3/4 tsp. ground cloves
2 (1-lb.) cans jellied cranberry sauce
1 qt. pineapple juice
Cinnamon sticks
Butter

In slow-cooking pot, combine brown sugar with water, salt, nutmeg, cinnamon, allspice, and cloves. Break up cranberry sauce with fork. Add cranberry sauce and pineapple juice to pot. Cover and heat on low for 3 to 4 hours. Serve hot in individual mugs with cinnamon sticks. Dot each mug with butter. Makes about 3 quarts.

MULLED CIDER

2 qts. apple cider
1/4 cup packed brown sugar
2 sticks cinnamon

1 tsp. whole cloves
1/8 tsp. ground ginger
1 orange, sliced (unpeeled)

Combine ingredients in slow-cooking pot. Cover and heat on low for 2 to 5 hours or longer. Serve from pot. Makes 10 to 12 servings.

PADRE PUNCH

1 (6-oz.) can frozen orange juice, partially
  thawed
3 orange juice cans water
1 qt. apple cider
5 whole cloves

2 cinnamon sticks
1 tsp. ground nutmeg
3/4 tsp. ground ginger
Orange slices

In slow-cooking pot, combine orange juice with water, cider, cloves, cinnamon, nutmeg and ginger. Cover and heat on low for 4 to 6 hours (or longer). Garnish with orange slices. Keep hot and serve punch in slow-cooking pot. Makes 7 to 10 servings. Recipe may be doubled if your slow-cooking pot is large enough.

BISHOP'S WINE

2 tbs. whole cloves
3 whole unpeeled oranges
2 (4/5-qt.) bottles dry red wine

1/2 cup sugar
1 stick cinnamon

Stick whole cloves into peel of whole oranges. Prick skin several times with fork. Drop into bottom of slow-cooking pot. Pour in wine, sugar, and cinnamon. Cover and cook on low for 3 to 4 hours. Serve hot from the pot. If desired, cut oranges into wedges as garnish for each serving. Makes 10 servings.

Hot Wine Cranberry Punch and Banana Nut Bread   Photo: Josh Young

West Bend 'Lazy Day' Slo-Cooker with **Mulled Cider**

APPLE BRANDY BREW

1 (4/5-qt.) bottle apple-flavored wine
2 cups apple cider

1 cup peach brandy
1 cinnamon stick

Combine ingredients in slow-cooking pot. Cover and heat on low for 3 to 4 hours. Serve hot. Makes 8 servings.

HOT WINE CRANBERRY PUNCH

1 pt. cranberry juice cocktail
1 cup water
3/4 cup sugar
2 sticks cinnamon

6 whole cloves
1 (4/5-qt.) bottle Burgundy wine
1 lemon, thinly sliced (unpeeled)

Combine ingredients in slow-cooking pot. Heat on low for 1 to 2 hours. Strain and serve hot. May be kept hot and served from slow-cooking pot set on lowest setting. Makes 6 to 8 mugs or 10 to 12 punch-cup servings.

SPICED APRICOT PUNCH

1 (46-oz.) can apricot nectar
3 cups orange juice
1/2 cup brown sugar, packed

2 tbs. lemon juice
3 sticks cinnamon
1/2 tsp. whole cloves

In slow-cooking pot, combine apricot nectar, orange juice, brown sugar, and lemon juice. Tie cinnamon and cloves in small cheesecloth bag; add to juices. Cover and heat on low for 2 to 5 hours. Serve hot from pot. Makes 12 servings.

HOT SPICY LEMONADE PUNCH

4 cups cranberry juice
2/3 cup sugar
1 (12-oz.) can lemonade concentrate, thawed
4 cups water

2 tbs. honey
6 whole cloves
2 cinnamon sticks, broken
1 lemon, sliced (unpeeled)

In slow-cooking pot, combine cranberry juice, sugar, lemonade concentrate, water and honey. Tie cloves and cinnamon in small cheesecloth square. Add spice bag and lemon slices to juices. Cover and cook on low for 3 to 4 hours. Remove spice bag. Keep hot in slow-cooking pot. Makes 9 to 10 cups.

HOT MINT MALT

6 chocolate-covered, cream-filled mint patties
5 cups milk
1/2 cup chocolate malted milk powder

1 tsp. vanilla
Whipped cream

In slow-cooking pot, combine mint patties with milk, malted milk powder, and vanilla. Heat on low for 2 hours. Beat with rotary beater until frothy. Pour into cups; top with whipped cream. Makes 6 servings.

SOUPS & SANDWICHES

After you have made a few soups, you will be convinced that slow cookers were made just for this purpose. They bring out the flavors by retaining all of the natural meat and vegetable juices.

If you are tired of rushing home after work or shopping to make dinner, plan to have a hearty main dish soup. Start with leftover turkey, chicken or ham bone. Then you can build almost any traditional soup with a few seasonings and vegetables. Put the ingredients into your slow cooker before you leave. When you get home, it will be ready to serve in large portions directly from the pot. To complete the meal, heat thick slices of buttered French bread. What could be easier?

Some soups are glamourous enough to serve your guests. *Green Vegetable Chowder* with sour cream added at the last minute is one example. *Bouillabaise* is quite a conversation piece in itself.

Notice how the cooking times vary for these soups. At such low temperatures most soups don't care if they are cooked longer. At the minimum recommended cooking time, lift the lid and stick a fork into the meat and several of the larger vegetable pieces to see whether they are done. Try not to keep the lid off any longer than necessary because steam and heat escape very fast. It takes a long time to replace the heat loss after you've replaced the lid.

Try some of the short-cut soups which start with a packaged mix or canned product as a base. They are surprisingly good and they take less cooking time than soups "made from scratch."

Slow cookers work fine as serving pots for hot sandwiches. *Sloppy Joes, Sloppy Janes* and *Chili Dogs* will be the favorites of the younger generation. You can combine the sandwich mixture in your slow cooker and leave it for several hours. Teenagers can serve themselves and make their own sandwiches or the Cub Scouts will devour it after their meeting.

Ham Stuffed Rolls and *Over-Stuffed Tuna Egg Sandwiches* can be completely assembled and kept warm in your pot. Don't plan to keep these sandwiches much longer than the suggested time because the bread will become soggy.

Dumpling Soup   Courtesy California Beef Council

DUMPLING SOUP

1 lb. beef stew meat, cut into 1-inch cubes
1 (1 3/8 oz.) pkg. onion soup mix
6 cups water, hot
2 carrots, peeled and shredded
1 stalk celery, finely chopped

1 tomato, peeled and chopped
1 cup packaged biscuit mix
1 tbs. finely chopped parsley
6 tbs. milk

In slow-cooking pot, sprinkle beef with dry onion soup mix. Pour hot water over meat. Stir in carrots, celery and tomato. Cover and cook on low for 4 to 6 hours or until meat is tender. Turn control on high. In small bowl, combine biscuit mix with parsley. Stir in milk with fork until mixture is moistened. Drop dumpling mixture into slow-cooking pot with a teaspoon. Cover and cook on high for 30 minutes. Makes 5-6 servings.

SHORT-CUT ITALIAN VEGETABLE SOUP

1 envelope country vegetable-with-noodles
  soup mix
2 cups boiling water
1 onion, chopped
2 carrots, peeled and chopped
1 (8-oz.) can tomato sauce

1 tsp. salt
1/8 tsp. pepper
1 (16-oz.) can kidney beans, drained
1 (16-oz.) can whole kernel corn, with liquid
Grated Parmesan cheese

Warm slow-cooking pot with hot tap water. In pot, stir dry soup mix into very hot water. Add onions, carrots, tomato sauce, salt and pepper. Cover and cook on low for 4 to 6 hours. Turn control to high; add beans and corn. Cover and cook on high for about 30 minutes. Sprinkle with cheese. Makes 4 to 6 servings.

HEARTY ALPHABET SOUP

1/2 lb. beef stew meat or round steak
1 (1-lb.) can stewed tomatoes
1 (8-oz.) can tomato sauce
1 cup water

1 package onion soup mix
1 (10-oz.) package frozen mixed vegetables,
  partially thawed
1/2 cup uncooked alphabet noodles

Cut beef into small cubes. In slow-cooking pot, combine meat with stewed tomatoes, tomato sauce, water, and soup mix. Cover and cook on low for 6 to 8 hours. Turn to high; add vegetables that have been partially thawed, and noodles. Cover and cook on high 30 minutes or until vegetables are done. Makes 5 to 6 servings.

TURKEY NOODLE SOUP*

1 turkey carcass, broken into several pieces
2 qts. water
1 tsp. salt
1/4 tsp. pepper
1 onion, chopped
2 stalks celery, chopped

1 carrot, chopped
1 tbs. dried parsley leaves
1/2 tsp. marjoram leaves
1 bay leaf
3-inch square cheesecloth
6 ozs. noodles, cooked and drained

Combine turkey carcass and water in slow-cooking pot. Add salt, pepper, onion, celery, and carrot. Place parsley, marjoram and bay leaf in center of cheesecloth. Gather up sides and tie. Drop in pot with turkey. Cover and cook on low for 5 to 6 hours. Remove carcass and spice bag from pot. Take meat off bones; return meat to broth. Drop cooked noodles into pot with meat. Cover and cook on high for 20 to 30 minutes. Makes 8 servings.

*This recipe is designed for a 4 1/2 quart slow-cooking pot. For 3 1/2 quart or smaller slow-cooking pots, use chunks of turkey meat cut off the bones, or chicken parts.

GEORGIA PEANUT SOUP

3 cups chicken broth or bouillon
1/4 cup finely chopped celery
1/4 tsp. salt
1 small onion, finely chopped
2 tbs. butter or margarine

1/2 cup peanut butter
1 cup milk or light cream
1/4 cup flour
1/4 cup water
1/4 cup finely chopped peanuts (optional)

Combine chicken stock, celery, salt, onion, butter, and peanut butter in slow-cooking pot. Cover and cook on high for 2 to 3 hours. Add milk and flour that has been dissolved in 1/4 cup water. Cook on high 15 minutes or until slightly thickened, stirring several times. Sprinkle peanuts over each serving, if desired. Makes 4 servings.

SWEDISH CABBAGE SOUP*

2 lamb shanks
2 beef bouillon cubes
1/2 tsp. pepper
1 tsp. salt
1 tbs. whole allspice
1 cup chopped leeks
1/2 cup peeled, diced parsnips

1 cup peeled, diced carrots
1/2 cup thinly sliced celery
2 medium potatoes, peeled and diced
1/4 cup minced parsley
2 qts. water
2 qts. shredded cabbage

Place lamb shanks in slow-cooking pot with bouillon cubes, pepper, and salt. Tie allspice in cheesecloth. Add allspice, leeks, parsnips, carrots, celery, potatoes, parsley, and water to pot. Cover and cook on low for 7 to 9 hours or until meat is tender. Remove allspice and meat from pot. Cut meat off bones; dice and return to pot. Skim off fat from top of soup. Turn control to high. Add cabbage. Cover and cook on high for 25 to 30 minutes or until cabbage is done. Makes 8 servings.

*This recipe designed for 4 1/2 quart or larger slow-cooking pot.

DOWN EAST CORN CHOWDER

3 cups fresh corn, cut from cob or 2 (16-oz.)
   cans whole kernel corn, drained
2 medium potatoes, peeled and finely
   chopped
1 onion, finely chopped
1 tsp. salt

1/2 tsp. seasoned salt
1/8 tsp. pepper
2 cups chicken broth or bouillon
2 cups milk
1/4 cup butter or margarine
Ground mace

Combine corn, potatoes, onion, salt, seasoned salt, pepper, and broth in slow-cooking pot. Cover and cook on low 7 to 9 hours. Pour into blender and puree until almost smooth. Chill overnight, if desired, or return to pot. Stir in milk and butter. Cover and cook on high for 1 hour. Pour into bowls; sprinkle with mace. Makes 6 to 8 servings.

Minestrone Soup   Courtesy Thermador

FRENCH ONION SOUP

3 large onions, thinly sliced
1/2 cup butter or margarine
2 tbs. instant beef bouillon or 6 bouillion
   cubes
4 cups hot water

1 tsp. Worcestershire sauce
1/2 tsp. salt
4 slices toasted French bread
1/4 cup grated Parmesan cheese

In large skillet or slow-cooking pot with browning unit, cook onions in butter until lightly browned. In pot, combine browned onions in butter with bouillon, water, Worcestershire sauce, and salt. Cover and cook on low 4 to 6 hours. Top each bowl with toasted French bread sprinkled with cheese. Makes 4 servings. Recipe may be doubled, kept hot in slow-cooking pot, and served from pot.

MINESTRONE SOUP

1 lb. beef shank or stew meat
6 cups water
1 onion, chopped
1 tsp. salt
1 tsp. powdered thyme
2 tbs. minced parsley
1/4 tsp. pepper

1 (16-oz.) can tomatoes, cut up
1 zucchini, thinly sliced
1 (16-oz.) can garbanzo beans, drained
2 cups chopped cabbage
1 cup small elbow macaroni, uncooked
1/4 cup grated Parmesan cheese

In slow-cooking pot, combine beef with water, onion, salt, thyme, parsley, pepper, and tomatoes. Cover and cook on low for 7 to 9 hours. Remove beef bones; cut up meat and return to pot. Turn control to high. Add zucchini, beans, cabbage, and macaroni. Cover and cook on high for 30 to 45 minutes or until vegetables are tender. Sprinkle with cheese. Makes 8 to 10 servings.

OLD FASHIONED VEGETABLE SOUP

2 lbs. soup bones or 1 lb. beef short ribs
2 qts. water
1 tsp. salt
1 tsp. celery salt
1 small onion, chopped
1 cup diced carrots

1/2 cup diced celery
2 cups diced potatoes
1 (1-lb.) can whole kernel corn, not drained
1 (1-lb.) can tomatoes, cut up
2 turnips, peeled and finely chopped

Place meat, water, salt, celery salt, onion, carrots, and celery in slow-cooking pot. Cover and cook on low 4 to 6 hours. Remove bones; chop meat and return to pot. Add potatoes, corn, tomatoes, and turnips. Cover and cook on high for 2 to 3 hours. Makes 8 to 10 servings.

Cream of Cauliflower Soup with Mushrooms   Courtesy Western Growers Association

CREAM OF CAULIFLOWER SOUP

1 medium head cauliflower, cut into
    flowerets
1 stalk celery, cut into 1-inch pieces
1 medium onion, chopped
1 tsp. salt

1/8 tsp. white pepper
1 qt. chicken or turkey broth
1 cup light cream
1/2 tsp. Worcestershire sauce
Nutmeg

Combine cauliflower, celery, onion, salt, pepper, and broth in slow-cooking pot. Cover and cook on low 6 to 8 hours. Force mixture through sieve or puree in blender. Return to pot. Add cream and Worcestershire sauce. Cook on high 5 to 10 minutes to heat. Sprinkle with nutmeg. Makes 6 servings.

GREEN VEGETABLE CHOWDER

6 to 8 medium leeks
2 small potatoes, peeled and diced
3 cups chicken broth or bouillon
1 (10-oz.) package frozen peas, thawed
1/2 cup coarsely chopped watercress leaves

2 tbs. butter
1 tsp. salt
1/2 tsp. seasoned salt
1/8 tsp. pepper
1/2 cup dairy sour cream

Trim and clean leeks; slice crosswise. In slow-cooking pot, combine leeks with potatoes, broth, peas, watercress, butter, salts, and pepper. Cover and cook on low 5 to 7 hours or until vegetables are tender. Pour 1/3 of mixture at a time into blender and whirl until smooth. Return mixture to pot. Turn control to high. Stir in sour cream; cook on high for 15 to 20 minutes or until hot. Spoon into bowls; garnish with a few watercress leaves. Makes 4 to 6 servings.

HERBED SPINACH SOUP

3 green onions, finely chopped
3 sprigs parsley
1/4 small head lettuce, sliced
1 bunch fresh spinach
2 tbs. butter or margarine
1/2 tsp. salt

1/8 tsp. pepper
1 tsp. tarragon
4 (10 1/2-oz.) cans beef consomme
1/2 cup light cream
1 hard-cooked egg, chopped

In slow-cooking pot, combine onions, parsley, lettuce, spinach, butter, salt, pepper, tarragon, and consomme. Cover and cook on low 4 to 6 hours. Pour into blender (part of the mixture at a time). Blend until vegetables are finely chopped. Turn slow-cooking pot on high. Pour blended mixture into pot. Stir in cream. Cook on high 20 to 30 minutes. Serve hot, with garnish of chopped hard-cooked egg. Makes 8 servings.

TAVERN SOUP

1/4 cup finely chopped celery
1/4 cup finely chopped carrot
1/4 cup finely chopped green pepper
1/4 cup finely chopped onion
3 (13 3/4-oz.) cans chicken broth
2 tbs. butter or margarine

1 tsp. salt
1/4 tsp. pepper
1/3 cup flour
3 cups (3/4 lb.) grated sharp cheddar cheese
1 (12-oz.) can light beer (at room temperature)

Combine celery, carrot, green pepper, and onion in slow-cooking pot. Add broth, butter, salt, and pepper. Cover and cook on low for 5 to 6 hours. Strain mixture; puree vegetables in blender and return to pot with broth. Turn control to high. Dissolve flour in small amount of water; add to broth. Add cheese, 1/2 cup at a time, stirring until blended. Pour in beer. Cover and cook on high 15 to 20 minutes. Makes 6 to 8 servings.

Beef Shank Soup   Courtesy California Beef Council

LENTIL SOUP—CRESCENTI STYLE*

1 to 2 lbs. beef neck bone or beef shanks
3 carrots, peeled and chopped
3 medium potatoes, peeled and chopped
1 large onion, peeled and chopped
3 stalks celery with tops, chopped
3 tomatoes, chopped
1/8 tsp. marjoram

5 cups water
5 beef bouillon cubes, crumbled
1/2 lb. lentils
1 tsp. salt
1/4 tsp. pepper
2 zucchini, chopped
1/2 head cabbage, shredded

In slow-cooking pot, combine beef with carrots, potatoes, onion, celery, tomatoes, marjoram, water, bouillon cubes, lentils, salt, and pepper. Cover and cook on low for 9 to 10 hours or until lentils are tender. Remove beef bones from pot; cut off meat and return to pot. Turn control to high. Add zucchini and cabbage. Cover pot and cook on high for 30 to 45 minutes or until vegetables are tender. Makes 8 servings. This is a thick, hearty soup, similar to a stew.

*This recipe designed for 4 1/2 quart or larger slow-cooking pot. Cut recipe in half for smaller pot.

SPLIT PEA SOUP

1 (1-lb.) package split peas
1 ham bone (with some meat left on) or
  2 ham hocks
1 carrot, diced
1 onion, diced

1 stalk celery, diced
2 qts. water
1 tsp. salt
1/4 tsp. pepper

Combine ingredients in slow-cooking pot. Cover and cook on low for 8 to 10 hours. Remove ham bone; cut meat off, dice, and return meat to soup. Makes 8 servings.

BEEF SHANK SOUP

1 to 1 1/2 lbs. beef shanks
8 cups water
1 onion, chopped
1/2 cup chopped celery
1 carrot, chopped
1 1/2 tsp. salt

2 tbs. finely chopped parsley
1 bay leaf
4 whole peppercorns
1 clove garlic, cut in half
1/4 tsp. dried thyme leaves
Cheesecloth (about 4-inch square)

In slow-cooking pot, combine beef with water, onion, celery, carrot, salt and parsley. Place bay leaf, peppercorns, thyme and garlic in center of cheesecloth. Pull up on each corner, forming a bag and tie. Drop in pot with meat. Cover and cook on low 6 to 8 hours, or until meat is tender. Remove spice bag. Ladle soup into bowls. Makes 6 to 8 servings.

This is a basic beef soup. For variations, before the last hour of cooking, add any one of the following: Two 1-lb. cans drained kidney beans and one sliced green pepper; or 3 cups cooked mixed vegetables; or 1 cup narrow uncooked noodles. Cover and cook for one hour.

NEW ENGLAND CLAM CHOWDER

1/4 lb. salt pork or bacon, cut in small cubes
1 onion, chopped
2 medium potatoes, peeled and diced
1/2 tsp. salt
1/8 tsp. pepper

3 cups water
2 (7-oz.) cans minced clams or 1 pint fresh-shucked clams, cut up
2 cups light cream or evaporated milk
Paprika

Saute pork with onion in a skillet or in slow-cooking pot with browning unit. Combine sauteed pork, onion, potatoes, salt, pepper, and water in pot. Cover and cook on low 5 to 7 hours. Turn control to high. Add clams and cream. Cover and cook on high for 15 minutes. Sprinkle with paprika. Makes 6 to 7 servings.

BOUILLABAISE

1 carrot, chopped
1 onion, chopped
1 clove garlic, minced
1 (1-lb.) can tomatoes, cut up
3 cups water
2 bay leaves
2 cups beef bouillon
1/4 cup chopped parsley

1/2 tsp. dried thyme leaves, crushed
1 tbs. salt
1 tsp. lemon juice
1/16 tsp. powdered saffron
1 lb. large uncooked shrimp, shelled
1 lb. fresh or frozen fish fillets, thawed and cut into 2-inch chunks
2 uncooked lobster tails, cut into 2-inch chunks*

In large slow-cooking pot, combine carrot, onion, garlic, tomatoes, water, bay leaves, bouillon, parsley, thyme, salt, lemon juice, and saffron. Cover and cook on low for 6 to 8 hours. Strain; return broth to pot. Turn control to high. Add shrimp, fish fillets, and lobster.* Cover pot and cook on high for 20 to 30 minutes or until seafood is done. Serve in large bowls with French bread. Makes 6 to 7 servings.

*If lobster tails are cooked, add them about 5 minutes before serving.

OVERSTUFFED TUNA-EGG SALAD ROLLS

1 (9 1/4-oz.) can tuna, drained
3 hard-cooked eggs, chopped
1/2 cup finely chopped celery
1 tbs. chopped chives
2 tbs. sweet pickle relish

1/2 cup mayonnaise
1/4 tsp. salt
1/8 tsp. pepper
6 to 7 hamburger buns
Foil

In mixing bowl, combine drained tuna, eggs, celery, chives, relish, mayonnaise, salt, and pepper. Spoon mixture into split hamburger buns. Wrap each bun in foil. Place in slow-cooking pot. Cover and heat on low for 2 to 2 1/2 hours. Serve hot from the pot. Makes 6 to 7 servings.

HOT CHICKEN SALAD

2 cups diced cooked chicken (or turkey)
1 1/2 cups diced celery
1 cup ham-flavored croutons
1/2 cup slivered toasted almonds
1 1/2 tsp. grated Parmesan cheese
4 tbs. mayonnaise

1 tbs. lemon juice
1/2 tsp. salt
1/4 tsp. curry powder (optional)
1 cup crushed potato chips
1/2 cup grated cheddar cheese

In slow-cooking pot, combine chicken, celery, croutons, almonds and Parmesan cheese. Toss together to mix. In small bowl, combine mayonnaise, lemon juice, salt and curry powder. Stir until well blended. Pour over chicken mixture. Stir to coat thoroughly. Cover and cook on low 2 to 3 hours. Sprinkle with potato chips and cheddar cheese. Turn to high and cook another 20 minutes or until cheese melts.

CHILI DOGS

1 (15-oz.) can chili with beans
1 (6-oz.) can tomato paste
1/4 cup minced green pepper
1/4 cup minced onion
1 tsp. prepared mustard

1/2 tsp. salt
1/2 tsp. chili powder
8 to 10 frankfurters
8 to 10 frankfurter buns

In slow-cooking pot, combine chili with beans, tomato paste, green pepper, onion, mustard, salt, and chili powder. Cover and cook on low for 3 to 4 hours. In large saucepan, drop frankfurters into boiling water; simmer several minutes. Toast buns. Serve a frankfurter on each bun. Spoon chili mixture onto frankfurters. Makes 8 to 10 servings.

Recipe may be doubled for a larger group. Keep chili mixture hot in slow-cooking pot. Serve from the pot.

SLOPPY JANE SANDWICHES

1 package (about 10) frankfurters, sliced
1 (28-oz.) can baked beans
1 tsp. prepared mustard

1 tsp. instant minced onion
1/3 cup chili sauce*
5 to 6 frankfurter buns, toasted

In slow-cooking pot, combine frankfurters with beans, mustard, onion, and chili sauce. Cover and cook on low for 2 to 3 hours. Spoon over toasted frankfurter buns. Makes 5 to 6 servings.

*Bottled tomato sauce similar to catsup.

BARBECUE BEEF SANDWICHES

2 cups thinly sliced cooked beef or pork
2 tbs. instant minced onion
1 tbs. brown sugar
2 tsp. paprika
1 tsp. crushed oregano
1 tsp. chili powder
1 tsp. cracked pepper
1/2 tsp. salt

1 bay leaf
1 clove garlic, minced
1 cup catsup
1/4 cup water
1 tbs. salad oil
1/4 cup tarragon vinegar
2 tbs. Worcestershire sauce
2 or 3 drops liquid smoke

Combine ingredients in slow-cooking pot. Cover and cook on low 4 to 6 hours. Remove and discard bay leaf. Serve hot over French rolls or buttered toast. Makes 4 to 5 servings.

SLOPPY JOES

1 1/2 lbs. lean ground beef
1 small onion, minced
2 stalks celery, minced
1 (12-oz.) bottle chili sauce*
2 tbs. brown sugar

1 tbs. Worcestershire sauce
1 tsp. salt
2 tbs. sweet pickle relish
1/8 tsp. pepper

In large skillet or slow-cooking pot with browning unit, cook beef with onion and celery until meat loses its red color. Pour off excess fat. In slow-cooking pot, combine meat, onion, and celery with remaining ingredients. Cover and cook on low for 3 to 4 hours. Spoon over toasted hamburger buns or French rolls. Makes 4 to 6 servings. Recipe may be doubled and mixture kept warm in slow-cooking pot for after-the-game party.

*Bottled tomato sauce similar to catsup.

REUBEN SANDWICHES

1 (1-lb.) can sauerkraut
Sliced corned beef brisket (not canned)*
1/4 lb. Swiss cheese, sliced

Sliced rye bread
Sandwich spread or Thousand Island dressing

Drain sauerkraut in sieve; then on paper towels until very dry. Place sauerkraut in bottom of slow-cooking pot. Arrange layer of corned beef slices on sauerkraut. Top with cheese slices. Cover and cook on low 3 to 4 hours. Toast slices of bread; spread generously with sandwich spread. Spoon ingredients from slow-cooking pot onto toasted bread, maintaining layers of sauerkraut, meat and cheese. Serve open-faced or closed. Makes three to four sandwiches.

*See recipe for Corned Beef.

HAM-STUFFED FRENCH ROLLS

2 cups finely chopped cooked ham
2 hard-cooked eggs, finely chopped
2 tbs. minced green onion
2 tbs. chopped ripe olives (optional)
1 tsp. prepared mustard

1 tsp. sweet pickle relish
1/2 cup small cubes cheddar cheese
1/3 cup mayonnaise
6 large or 8 small French rolls

Combine ham with eggs, onion, olives, mustard, relish, cheese, and mayonnaise. Cut off tops *or* one end of rolls; scoop out most of soft center. Fill with ham mixture. Replace top or end of roll. Place filled rolls in slow-cooking pot. Cover and heat on low for 2 to 3 hours. Rolls may be kept hot and served from the pot. Makes 6 to 8 servings.

WELSH RAREBIT

1 (12-oz.) can beer
1 tbs. dry mustard
1 tsp. Worcestershire sauce
1/2 tsp. salt

1/8 tsp. pepper
1 lb. processed American cheese, cut into cubes
1 lb. sharp cheddar cheese, cut into cubes

In slow-cooking pot, combine beer, mustard, Worcestershire sauce, salt and pepper. Cover and cook on high for 1 to 2 hours or until mixture boils. Add cheese a little at a time, stirring constantly, until all cheese has melted. Heat on high for 20 to 30 minutes with lid off, stirring frequently. Serve hot over toast or toasted English muffins. Garnish with strips of crisp bacon and tomato slices. Makes 4 to 6 servings.

MAIN DISHES

Every family has a few favorite meal-in-one dishes. Just add a salad and you have a complete meal. Slow-cooking pots are perfect for such meals because you can combine most of the ingredients and let them cook while you are busy on another project.

I have included a few classics and popular combination dishes which lend themselves admirably to slow cooking. Several of these feature fish or seafood. Because most fish or seafood should be cooked quickly, it is not suitable for slow cooking. For this reason, you should use your pot for sauce-making. Put vegetables and seasonings in your slow cooker and add the seafood at the end of the cooking time. *Paella in a Pot* is a good example of this. It is quite an exotic dish to make—and you can serve it directly from the pot. But—the fish and rice are added at the very last part of the cooking session.

Rice is not at its best when cooked longer than recommended on the package. Cook it first, then add to the pot a short time before serving.

The same principle applies to most pasta—macaroni and spaghetti products. They provide real added taste pleasure without straining the budget. When fixing pasta, remember that sauce flavors are enhanced by long times in the slow cooker, but the pasta should be added near the end of the cooking time.

Another point to remember is to add cheese, milk, cream and sour cream shortly before serving. Dairy products are at their best when refrigerated as long as possible, then added for flavor, texture and nutrition near the end of the cooking period or served with the food.

If you want a creamy sauce for a main dish, cook the vegetables, spices and meats in water, bouillon or tomato sauce for a special flavor. Then add the cream or milk and thicken later.

Follow all of these main dish suggestions and you will be able to experiment on your own. Don't forget the versatility of packaged seasoning mixes which blend well with many Italian and Mexican-type dishes. You will discover countless variations and combinations you can tailor-make for your family.

JAMBALAYA

1 broiler-fryer chicken, cut up
3 onions, chopped
1 carrot, sliced
1 clove garlic, minced
1/2 tsp. oregano
1/2 tsp. basil

1 tsp. salt
1/8 tsp. pepper
1 (14-oz.) can tomatoes, cut up
1 lb. shelled, raw shrimp
2 cups cooked rice

In slow-cooking pot, combine chicken with onions, carrots, garlic, oregano, basil, salt, pepper and tomatoes. Cover and cook on low 4 to 5 hours. Turn control to high. Add shrimp and rice. Cover and cook on high for 30 to 40 minutes or until shrimp is done. Makes 5 to 6 servings.

1/Here's how to shell shrimp. Hold tail firmly in one hand. With other hand separate legs with thumb and peel back the shell. Snap off the tail.

2/Distribute chicken and vegetables in slow-cooking pot.

SHRIMP MARINARA

1 (16-oz.) can peeled tomatoes, cut up
2 tbs. minced parsley
1 clove garlic, minced
1/2 tsp. dried basil
1 tsp. salt
1/4 tsp. pepper

1 tsp. dried oregano
1 (6-oz.) can tomato paste
1/2 tsp. seasoned salt
1 lb. cooked shelled shrimp
Grated Parmesan cheese
Cooked spaghetti

In slow-cooking pot, combine tomatoes with parsley, garlic, basil, salt, pepper, oregano, tomato paste, and seasoned salt. Cover and cook on low 6 to 7 hours. Turn control to high. Stir in shrimp; cover and cook on high for 10 to 15 minutes. Serve, topped with Parmesan cheese, over cooked spaghetti. Makes 4 servings.

PAELLA IN A POT

1 (2 1/2 to 3-lb.) frying chicken, cut up
2 carrots, cut into sticks
2 onions, cut into eighths
1 (13 3/4-oz.) can chicken broth
1 clove garlic, minced
2 tbs. chopped pimiento

1/2 tsp. salt
1/4 tsp. ground oregano
1/16 tsp. saffron powder
2 cups cooked rice
1/2 lb. shelled raw shrimp
12 small clams in shells

In slow-cooking pot, combine chicken with carrots, onions, broth, garlic, pimiento, salt, oregano, and saffron. Cover and cook on low for 4 to 6 hours. Turn control to high. Add cooked rice, shrimp, and clams. Cover and cook on high for another 30 to 50 minutes or until shrimp is done. Makes 6 to 8 servings.

SHELL CASSEROLE

1 lb. lean ground beef
1 small onion, chopped
1 tsp. salt
1/4 tsp. garlic powder
1 tsp. Worcestershire sauce
1/4 cup flour

1 1/4 cups hot water
2 tsp. beef bouillon
2 tbs. red wine
6 ozs. large shell-shaped macaroni
1 (2-oz.) can sliced mushrooms, drained
1 cup dairy sour cream

In skillet or slow-cooking pot with browning unit, cook ground beef and onion until red color disappears. Drain meat; place in slow-cooking pot. Stir in salt, garlic powder, Worcestershire sauce and flour. Add water, bouillon and wine; mix well. Cover and cook on low for 2 to 3 hours. In meantime, cook macaroni according to package directions. Add cooked macaroni, mushrooms and sour cream to slow-cooking pot; stir to mix ingredients. Cover and cook on high for 10 to 15 minutes. Makes 4 to 5 servings.

MOCK CHILI RELLENO

2 tsp. butter
1 (4-oz.) can whole green chilies
1/2 lb. grated cheddar cheese
1/2 lb. grated Monterey Jack cheese

1 (14 1/2-oz.) can tomato slices, drained
4 eggs
3/4 cup evaporated milk
2 tbs. flour

Grease sides and bottom of slow-cooking pot with butter. Remove seeds from chilies; cut into strips. Place half the chilies in bottom of pot. Layer with cheddar cheese, then rest of chilies, Jack cheese, and tomatoes. Separate eggs. Beat whites until stiff. Fold in slightly beaten yolks and milk. Add flour. Pour over top of tomatoes. Cover and cook on high for 2 to 3 hours. Serve while piping hot. Makes 4 to 5 servings.

TORTILLA PIE

1 1/2 lbs. lean ground beef
1 package enchilada sauce mix
2 (8-oz.) cans tomato sauce
1/2 tsp. salt
1 cup water

1 large onion, finely chopped
1 (2 1/4-oz.) can sliced, ripe olives
Heavy-duty foil (about 15 inches long)
8 to 10 corn tortillas
1 cup grated cheddar cheese

Sauce:
1 (8-oz.) can tomato sauce
1/2 cup water

1 package spicy cheese dip mix (about 1/2 oz.)

In skillet or slow-cooking pot with browning unit, cook beef until crumbly; drain off excess fat. In mixing bowl, combine dry enchilada sauce mix with tomato sauce, salt, and water; stir in onion, olives, and browned beef. Line slow-cooking pot with foil by making a "nest" in the bottom. Spoon 2 tbs. meat-sauce mixture on foil in bottom. Arrange alternate layers of tortillas and meat sauce, ending with a layer of sauce on top. Cover and cook on low for 4 to 6 hours. Sprinkle with cheese. Cook another 5 minutes. Picking up sides of foil liner, lift tortilla pie out of pot. Slide onto serving dish. Cut into wedges; serve with sauce. Makes 6 servings.

Sauce: In small saucepan, combine tomato sauce, water, and dry cheese dip mix. Cover and simmer for 5 minutes. Serve hot.

CALIFORNIA TAMALE PIE

1 lb. lean ground beef
3/4 cup yellow corn meal
1 1/2 cups milk
1 egg, beaten
1 package chili seasoning mix

1 tsp. seasoned salt
1 (1-lb.) can tomatoes, cut up
1 (1-lb.) can whole kernel corn, drained
1 (2 1/4-oz.) can sliced ripe olives, drained
1 cup grated cheddar cheese

In skillet or slow-cooking pot with browning unit, cook meat until crumbly; drain. In large bowl, mix corn meal, milk, and egg. Add drained meat, dry chili seasoning mix, seasoned salt, tomatoes, corn, and olives. Pour into slow-cooking pot. Cover and cook on high for 3 to 4 hours. Sprinkle cheese over top. Cook another 5 minutes. Makes 6 to 8 servings.

MOIST CORNBREAD

3 eggs
2 cups milk

2 tbs. melted butter
1 (15-oz.) pkg. cornbread mix

Beat eggs in medium bowl; beat in milk, butter and cornbread mix. Pour into greased 8-cup baking dish or spring-form pan. Place in slow-cooking pot and cover with several paper towels. Cover and cook on high for 2 to 3 hours.

VEGETARIAN SPAGHETTI

1 package spaghetti sauce mix
1 (8-oz.) can tomato sauce
1 cup water
4 zucchini
1 small eggplant

1 small green pepper, cut into 1-inch cubes
3 medium tomatoes, cut into small wedges
1/2 tsp. salt
1/2 lb. uncooked spaghetti
1/4 lb. mozzarella cheese, grated

In slow-cooking pot, mix dry spaghetti sauce mix with tomato sauce and water. Cut zucchini into 1/2-inch crosswise slices. Peel eggplant; slice thinly, then cut each slice into quarters. Add zucchini, eggplant, green pepper, tomatoes, and salt to spaghetti sauce. Cover and cook on low for 4 to 6 hours or until vegetables are tender. In meantime, cook spaghetti according to package directions; drain well. When ready to serve, top each serving of spaghetti with vegetable-sauce mixture. Sprinkle with cheese. May be served as main dish or as accompaniment to thinly sliced roast beef. Makes 6 servings.

CHEESE FONDUE

1 lb. natural Swiss cheese, shredded
6 oz. natural or process Gruyere cheese,
  shredded
2 tsp. cornstarch

1 clove garlic, halved
1 1/3 cups sauterne wine
1 tbs. lemon juice
French bread, cut into bite-size chunks

Combine Swiss and Gruyere cheese with cornstarch. Rub inside of slow-cooking pot with cut garlic; then discard garlic. Pour sauterne and lemon juice into pot; turn control on high. Heat for 20 to 30 minutes or until very hot. Gradually add cheese (a handful at a time) stirring constantly until melted. After cheese is completely melted, turn control to low to keep warm. Dip chunks of French bread into hot fondue. If fondue gets too thick, turn to high, add one or two extra tablespoons of warmed sauterne and stir until blended. Makes 8 to 10 servings.

DAD'S HAM & POTATOES

4 or 5 baking potatoes
1/4 cup butter or margarine
1/4 cup flour
1/2 tsp. salt

2 cups milk or light cream
1/2 tsp. Worcestershire sauce
2 cups cooked ham, cut into chunks
1/2 cup grated cheddar cheese

Wash potatoes; drain but do not dry. Place in slow-cooking pot. Cover and cook on low for 6 to 8 hours. Cool slightly.* Peel and slice. In saucepan, melt butter. Add flour and salt; stir until blended. Slowly add milk, stirring constantly. Cook several minutes, stirring until smooth and thickened. Stir in Worcestershire sauce, then potatoes and ham. Spoon into 1 1/2-qt. baking dish. Sprinkle with cheese. Heat in 350°F. oven for 30 to 40 minutes. Makes 4 to 5 servings. This recipe not suitable for Cornwall or Sears tray-type Crockery Cookers.

*At this point, potatoes may be refrigerated and the recipe continued the next day, if desired.

BEANS

Because slow cookers are up-to-date electric cousins of the old-fashioned bean pot, bean dishes cook fine in them. Modern-day homemakers like to prepare beans in slow cookers because they can spend the day away from home while long, slow cooking is mingling compatible flavors to create the old-fashioned taste of Grandmother's bean pot.

Directions for cooking dried beans suggest the long-soaking method. If it is inconvenient for you to soak beans overnight, you can add six cups of water to one pound of beans. Bring to a boil and simmer two minutes. Remove from heat, cover and let stand one hour. Then follow the directions for cooking each bean recipe. If you live at a high altitude, boil the beans first, then let them soak overnight in the same water before cooking.

Most bean recipes may be cooked longer than the times indicated or they may be cooked one day and re-heated in the slow cooker for use the next day.

If you like your beans saucy, don't pour off any of the liquid in which the beans were soaked—leave as much juice in the pot as possible during the long cooking process.

Most of the bean recipes serve 6 to 8 people. If you have a 4 1/2 quart or larger slow cooker, you can double any of these recipes for a party. While you are getting everything else ready, the beans cook with no fuss or bother. Then they stay hot until serving time in a slow cooker. In case you hadn't guessed— slow cookers are ideal buffet servers.

CONGRESSIONAL BEAN SOUP

1 lb. dried small white beans*
8 cups water
1 meaty ham bone or 2 cups diced cooked
   ham
1 cup finely chopped celery

1 onion, finely chopped
2 tbs. finely chopped parsley
1 tsp. salt
1/4 tsp. pepper
1 bay leaf

In large pan, heat beans in water. Boil gently for 2 minutes; turn off heat and let stand 1 hour. Pour into slow-cooking pot. Add remaining ingredients. Cover and cook on low for 12 to 14 hours or until beans are very soft. Remove bay leaf and ham bone. Cut meat off bone; return meat to beans. Serve hot. Makes 6 to 8 servings.

*May be soaked overnight if preferred.

PORTUGUESE BEAN SOUP

1 cup dried red beans
6 cups water
2 onions, sliced
1 clove garlic, minced
1/4 lb. salt pork, cut into thick slices

3 potatoes, peeled and diced
1/4 tsp. allspice
1 (8-oz.) can tomato paste
1 tsp. salt
3 tsp. beef bouillon, or 3 bouillon cubes

In slow-cooking pot, soak beans in water overnight. Cover and cook on high for 2 to 3 hours or until tender. Add remaining ingredients. Cover and cook on low for 6 to 8 hours. Makes 6 to 8 servings.

BAKED BEAN SOUP

1 (1-lb. 12-oz.) can baked beans
6 slices cooked bacon, chopped
2 tbs. bacon drippings
2 tbs. finely chopped onion

1 (1-lb.) can stewed tomatoes
1 tbs. brown sugar
1 tbs. vinegar
1 tsp. seasoned salt

Combine all ingredients in slow-cooking pot. Cover and cook on low for 4 to 6 hours. Makes 5 to 6 servings.

Boston Baked Beans   Courtesy California Dry Bean Advisory Board

144 Beans

BOSTON BAKED BEANS

1 lb. dried small white beans
6 cups water
1 tsp. salt
1/2 cup molasses

2 tsp. dry mustard
1/4 cup brown sugar
1 medium onion, chopped
1/4 lb. salt pork

Pour beans into slow-cooking pot; add water. Soak overnight or at least 6 hours. Cover pot and cook on high for 2 to 3 hours or until beans are tender. Drain, saving liquid. Mix 1 cup of the liquid with salt, molasses, mustard, brown sugar and onion. Cut salt pork into 2 or 3 pieces. In slow-cooking pot, combine drained beans with molasses mixture and pork. Cover and cook on low for 10 to 12 hours. Keep hot in slow-cooking pot, using it as serving dish. Makes 6 to 8 servings.

VERMONT BAKED BEANS WITH HAM

1 lb. dried baby lima beans
6 cups water
2 cups diced baked ham or 2 ham hocks
1 tbs. prepared mustard

1/2 cup brown sugar
1/2 cup maple-flavored syrup
1 tsp. salt
1/4 tsp. pepper

Soak beans in water overnight in slow-cooking pot. Cover and cook on high for 2 to 3 hours or until tender but not mushy. Drain, saving liquid. Return beans to slow-cooking pot. Stir in ham, mustard, brown sugar, maple syrup, salt, pepper, and 1/2 cup liquid from beans. Cover and cook on low for 8 to 10 hours. If using ham hocks, cut ham off bones. Return meat to beans. Makes 6 servings.

SOUR CREAM LIMAS

1 lb. dried baby lima beans
6 cups water
1/4 cup melted butter
1/2 cup brown sugar

1/4 cup molasses
2 tbs. prepared mustard
1 tsp. salt
1 cup dairy sour cream

Soak beans in water overnight. Cook in slow-cooking pot on high for 2 to 3 hours, or until tender. Drain thoroughly; pour beans into large mixing bowl. Combine butter, brown sugar, molasses, mustard and salt. Mix with drained beans. Stir in sour cream. Spoon into baking dish. Heat in 350°F. oven for 30 to 40 minutes or until bubbly. Makes 6 to 8 servings.

BAKED BEAN CASSOULET

1 lb. dried red or kidney beans
6 cups water
1 medium onion, chopped
1/4 cup molasses
1 (15-oz.) can tomato sauce
1 tsp. salt

1/4 tsp. dry mustard
1/8 tsp. pepper
1 tbs. Worcestershire sauce
1 (12-oz.) pkg. smoked sausage links, cut into
    1-inch slices

In slow-cooking pot, soak beans in water overnight. Cover and cook on high for 2 to 3 hours or until tender. Drain, saving liquid. Combine 1 cup of the liquid with onion, molasses, tomato sauce, salt, mustard, pepper and Worcestershire sauce. Mix with drained beans in slow-cooking pot. Cover and cook on low for 10 to 12 hours. Add sausage the last hour of cooking. Makes 6 to 8 servings.

PIZZA BEANS

1 lb. pinto beans
6 cups water
4 medium tomatoes, peeled and diced
1 onion, chopped
1/4 cup chopped green pepper
1 clove garlic, crushed

2 tsp. salt
1/2 tsp. oregano leaves, crushed
1/4 tsp. rosemary, crushed
1 cup shredded mozzarella cheese
1/4 cup grated Romano or Parmesan cheese

Soak beans in water overnight. In slow-cooking pot, cook soaked beans in water on high for 2 to 3 hours, or until tender but not mushy. Drain, saving liquid. In slow-cooking pot, combine beans with tomatoes, onion, green pepper, garlic, salt, oregano, and rosemary. Add 2 cups liquid from beans. Cover and cook on low for 8 to 10 hours. Turn control to high; add mozzarella and Romano cheeses. Cook, uncovered, on high for 15 to 20 minutes. Turn heat off; let stand a few minutes before serving to let beans absorb some of the juice. Makes 6 to 8 servings.

SOUTHWESTERN HAM & BEANS

1 lb. dried pinto beans
Water

4 small dried chilies
2 medium ham hocks

In slow-cooking pot, cover pinto beans with water. Soak for about 12 hours. Drain water; re-cover with water. Add chilies. Cover and cook on low for 10 to 12 hours. Add ham hocks; cover and cook on low another 10 to 12 hours. Remove rind and bone from ham hocks; cut meat into small pieces and return to pot with beans. Mix well. Makes 6 to 8 servings.

RANCH STYLE BEANS

1 lb. lean ground beef
1 envelope green onion dip mix
2 (16-oz.) cans pork and beans in tomato
  sauce

1 (16-oz.) can kidney beans, drained
1 cup catsup
2 tbs. prepared mustard
2 tsp. vinegar

In large skillet or slow-cooking pot with browning unit, cook meat until red color disappears. Drain off excess fat. In slow-cooking pot, combine beef, dry dip mix, undrained pork and beans, drained kidney beans, catsup, mustard, and vinegar. Cover and cook on low for 3 to 4 hours. Makes 8 servings.

ZIPPY BEANS AND HOMINY

2 slices bacon, cooked and drained
1 (7-oz.) can green chili salsa
2 tsp. prepared mustard

1 tsp. Worcestershire sauce
1 (1-lb.) can kidney beans, drained
1 (1-lb.) can yellow hominy, drained

Combine ingredients in slow-cooking pot. Cover and cook on low for 4 to 5 hours. Serve. Especially good with barbecued hamburgers. Makes 6 servings.

SWEET-SOUR BEAN TRIO

4 slices bacon
1 onion, chopped
1/4 cup brown sugar
1 tsp. prepared mustard
1 clove garlic, crushed

1 tsp. salt
1/4 cup vinegar
1 (1-lb.) can lima beans, drained
1 (1-lb.) can baked beans, drained
1 (1-lb.) can kidney beans, drained

Cook bacon in skillet or slow-cooking pot with browning unit. Crumble bacon. Combine cooked bacon and 2 tbs. bacon drippings with onion, brown sugar, mustard, garlic, salt and vinegar. Mix with three kinds of beans in slow-cooking pot. Cover and cook on low for 6 to 8 hours. Makes 6 to 8 servings.

SAVORY TOMATO LIMAS

2 cups (1 lb.) large dry lima beans
6 cups water
1 onion, chopped
1 clove garlic, minced
1 tbs. prepared mustard
1 tbs. Worcestershire sauce

1 tsp. salt
1/2 tsp. chili powder
1 (10 1/2-oz.) can condensed tomato soup
2 tbs. vinegar
2 tbs. brown sugar
1/4 lb. salt pork, cut into several pieces

Soak beans in water overnight. Pour into slow-cooking pot. Cover and cook on high for 2 hours. Drain. Combine onion, garlic, mustard, Worcestershire sauce, salt, chili powder, tomato soup, vinegar, and sugar. Mix with beans in slow-cooking pot. Top with pork. Cover and cook on low for 9 to 11 hours. Makes 8 servings.

MAC'S KIDNEY BEANS

4 slices bacon, chopped
3 (15-oz.) cans kidney beans, drained
1 cup chili sauce*

1/2 cup sliced green onions
1/3 cup brown sugar

In small skillet, cook bacon, saving 2 tbs. drippings. In slow-cooking pot, add bacon and 2 tbs. bacon drippings to drained kidney beans, chili sauce and green onions. Sprinkle top with brown sugar. Cover pot and cook on low for 4 to 6 hours. Keep beans hot and serve from pot. Makes 8 to 10 servings.

*Bottled tomato sauce similar to catsup.

BLACK EYED PEAS, MEXICAN STYLE

1 lb. dried black-eyed peas
6 cups water
1/4 lb. salt pork, cut into thick slices
1 clove garlic, minced

1 tsp. salt
1/4 tsp. pepper
1/4 tsp. dried oregano

In slow-cooking pot combine black-eyed peas with water. Soak overnight. Cook soaked beans in water on high for 2 to 2 1/2 hours or until tender, but not mushy. Turn control on low. Stir in salt pork, garlic, salt, pepper and oregano. Cover and cook on low 8 to 10 hours. Drain and serve.

Mexican Style Black Eyed Peas   Courtesy California Dry Bean Advisory Board

BREADS & CAKES

If you think it takes a genius to bake breads or cakes in a slow cooker, give some of these recipes a try so you can tell your friends how easy it is.

There are a few tricks to remember when "baking" in one of these pots. First, turn the control to HIGH (or to the setting which is equivalent to the HIGH used in my recipes). The LOW setting is too low to give breads and cakes the texture you expect. With breads, remember to cover the container with a lid or foil. Tie the lid or foil onto the container and place the container on a metal rack or trivet inside the pot. If you don't have a metal rack or trivet to fit your slow cooker, crumple foil and place it in the bottom of the pot to support the baking container. Pour 2 cups of hot water around the container to provide steam for cooking the bread. You do not need to use a rack, add water, or cover the baking container in the West Bend Slo-Cooker Plus. Heat setting 5 is recommended for baking.

When using a deep-fryer type slow cooker, check frequently to make sure the water hasn't evaporated. Add more water if needed.

As a rule, it is not a good idea to remove the lid or foil from the bread container during the first 2 hours of cooking. After that, check the bread by inserting a toothpick in the mixture. If the toothpick comes out clean, the bread is done.

When using a standard cake mix, as in the recipe for *Banana Nut Cake* or *Applesauce Spice Cake,* the procedure is slightly different. Cakes are "baked" in a pan set directly on the bottom of the slow cooker, similar to the way you would do it in an oven. It is not necessary to use a trivet or water. Instead of covering the uncooked cake mixture with foil or a lid, cover the top with four or five layers of paper towels. Because there is more moisture in a slow cooker than in an oven it is necessary to compensate for this with the paper towels to help absorb the moist top of the cake mix. Also, leave the lid of your slow cooker slightly open to let extra moisture escape.

Try the *Plum Pudding!* It is cooked in a mold inside your slow cooker. This recipe calls for a metal rack or trivet for the mold and warm water around it. The water helps to steam the pudding, giving a moist texture to all its yummy spices and fruits.

The type and kind of container to use for breads and cakes will depend on the size of your pot. In addition to molds and coffee cans, spring forms or small bundt pans make excellent containers. The following containers hold approximately the same amount of batter so you can substitute one for another:

1 (2-lb.) coffee can	6- or 7-cup mold
2 (1-lb.) coffee cans	1 1/2-quart baking dish
3 (16-oz.) vegetable cans	

Many different containers work well for baking. Here two souffle dishes do the trick.

Spring form pans work well, as do coffee cans and cake molds.

Oster Super Pot is large enough to hold a tube pan.

Cover pan or mold with foil for steam baking.

Tie foil tightly to keep bread dry when steam baking.

Place trivet or meat rack in bottom of pot to keep pan out of water for steam baking.

Place pan or mold on rack. Pour about 2 cups of water in bottom of pot. Water should be just below baking container. Cover and cook on HIGH.

To bake a regular cake mix, place pan directly on bottom of pot. Put 4 to 5 paper towels on top of pan to absorb extra moisture. Cover and cook on HIGH. For this dry baking method, no water is used around pan.

SLOW-COOKING POTS	2 (1-lb.) Coffee Cans	1 (2-lb.) Coffee Can	3 (15-oz.) or (16-oz.) Vegetable Cans	4-cup Mold	7-cup Mold*	9-cup Mold*	8-inch Spring-Form Pan
Cornwall 4-Quart**			X	X	X		
Cornwall 4 1/2-Quart			X	X	X	X	
Cornwall 8-Quart	X		X	X	X	X	X
Dominion Crock-A-Dial			X	X	X		
Farberware 5-Quart		X		X	X	X	X
Grandinetti 3 1/2-Quart			X	X	X		
Grandinetti 5-Quart	X		X	X	X	X	X
Hamilton Beach Crock-Watcher			X	X	X		
Hamilton Beach Simmer-on			X	X	X		
Nesco Pot Luck Cooker			X	X	X	X	
Oster 8-Quart Super Pot	X		X	X	X	X	X
Penneys Slow Cooker/Fryer		X	X	X	X	X	
Presto 5-Quart				X	X	X	X
Regal Pot O' Plenty	X		X	X	X	X	
Rival 3 1/2-Quart Crock-Pot			X	X	X		
Rival 4 1/2-Quart Crock-Pot	X		X	X	X	X	X
Sears 4-Quart**			X	X	X		
Sears 5-Quart			X		X	X	
Sunbeam Crocker-Cooker-Fryer		X	X	X	X	X	
West Bend Lazy Day Slo-Cooker	X		X	X	X	X	

West Bend Slo-Cooker Plus. Use 9" x 5" loaf pan
* 7- and 9-cup molds are not always shaped the same.
** Integrated model (crockery pot and heating unit combined).

POUND CAKE

1 (16-oz.) pkg. pound cake mix   2 eggs
2/3 cup water

Blend cake mix with water and eggs in mixing bowl on low speed until moistened. Beat on medium speed for 3 minutes, scraping the bowl frequently. Pour into a greased and floured 8-cup mold or spring form pan. Place in slow-cooking pot. Cover mold with 4 or 5 paper towels. Cover pot and cook on high 2 1/2 to 3 1/2 hours. When cake is done, top will be slightly moist and a toothpick inserted in the center comes out clean. Cool on rack 5 minutes before removing cake from pan. Turn out of pan and cool. Serve plain, frosted or with fruit. Makes 6 servings.

BOSTON BROWN BREAD

1 cup corn meal
1 cup rye flour
1 1/2 tsp. baking soda
1 tsp. salt

1 cup whole wheat flour
3/4 cup molasses
2 cups sour milk or buttermilk
1 cup raisins

In large bowl, combine corn meal, rye flour, soda, and salt; add wheat flour. In small bowl, stir molasses into sour milk; add to dry ingredients, a little at a time. Stir just enough to blend. Add raisins. Spoon into two greased (1-lb.) coffee cans. Cover with foil; tie. Place cans on metal rack in bottom of slow-cooking pot. Pour 2 cups hot water around cans. Cover pot and cook on high for 2 1/2 to 3 hours. Remove cans from pot. Let stand 5 to 10 minutes. Turn bread out on cooling rack. Serve warm with butter.

GINGER BROWN BREAD

1 (14-oz.) pkg. gingerbread mix
1/4 cup yellow corn meal
1 tsp. salt

1 1/2 cups milk
1/2 cup raisins

Combine gingerbread mix with corn meal and salt in large bowl; stir in milk until mixture is evenly moist. Beat at medium speed with electric mixer for 2 minutes. Stir in raisins. Pour into greased and floured 6 or 7-cup mold. Cover with foil; tie. Put trivet or metal rack in slow-cooking pot. Pour 2 cups hot water in pot. Place filled mold on rack or trivet. Cover pot and cook on high for 3 to 4 hours or until bread is done. Remove from pot; cool on rack 5 minutes. Loosen edges with knife; turn out on rack and cool slightly. Serve warm with butter or cream cheese.

STEAMED MOLASSES BREAD

2 cups all-bran cereal
2 cups whole wheat flour
2 tsp. baking powder
1 tsp. salt
1 tsp. baking soda

1 cup raisins
1 egg
1 3/4 cups sour milk or buttermilk
1/2 cup dark molasses

In medium bowl, combine bran, flour, baking powder, salt, baking soda, and raisins. In another bowl, beat the egg; add sour milk and molasses. Blend in dry ingredients; do not overbeat. Pour into greased and floured 8-cup mold or can. Cover with foil; tie. Place rack in slow-cooking pot. Pour 2 cups hot water in pot. Place covered bread container on rack. Cover pot and cook on high for 3 to 4 hours. Turn bread out on cooling rack. Serve warm or cool.

PEANUT BUTTER LOAF

3/4 cup hot water
3/4 cup peanut butter
3/4 cup milk
1/2 tsp. sugar
1/4 tsp. salt

1 egg
2 cups flour
4 tsp. baking powder
3/4 cup chopped salted peanuts

In large bowl, pour hot water over peanut butter. Stir in milk, sugar, salt, egg, flour, and baking powder. Mix well. Add peanuts. Grease 5 or 6-cup mold. Spoon bread mixture into mold. Cover with foil and tie. Place mold on rack in slow-cooking pot. Pour 2 cups hot water around mold. Cover pot and cook on high for 2 to 3 hours or until done. Remove from pot. Let bread stand in mold for 10 minutes; turn out on cooling rack. Serve warm or cool; spread with butter, marmalade, or jam.

CRANBERRY NUT BREAD

2 cups (1/2 lb.) fresh cranberries
1 medium cooking apple, peeled, cored, and
   cut into chunks
1/2 cup walnuts
2 cups flour
1 cup sugar
1 1/2 tsp. baking powder

1/2 tsp. baking soda
1/2 tsp. salt
6 tbs. soft butter
1 egg
1 tbs. grated orange peel
1/2 cup orange juice

Put cranberries, apple, and walnuts through coarsest blade of food grinder; set aside. Combine flour, sugar, baking powder, baking soda, and salt in a deep bowl. Cut in butter until size of peas. Stir in egg, orange peel, and juice; then the cranberry-apple mixture. Stir until blended. Spoon into greased 2-qt. mold or two 1-lb. coffee cans. Cover with foil and tie. Place filled mold or coffee cans on metal rack in slow-cooking pot. Pour 2 cups hot water around mold. Cover pot and cook on high for 2 1/2 to 3 hours. Remove mold from pot. Let stand several minutes; turn bread out on cooling rack. Serve warm with butter. Especially good as a coffee cake for brunch; with fresh fruit plate, or chicken salad for lunch.

BANANA NUT BREAD

1/3 cup shortening
1/2 cup sugar
2 eggs
1 3/4 cups all-purpose flour
1 tsp. baking powder

1/2 tsp. baking soda
1/2 tsp. salt
1 cup mashed ripe bananas
1/2 cup chopped walnuts

Cream together shortening and sugar; add eggs and beat well. Sift dry ingredients; add to creamed mixture alternately with banana, blending well after each addition. Stir in nuts. Pour into well-greased 4 to 6-cup mold. Cover with foil and tie. Pour 2 cups hot water in slow-cooking pot. Place mold on rack or trivet in pot. Cover and cook on high 2 to 3 hours or until bread is done. Serve warm or cool, with butter, peanut butter or cream cheese.

DATE AND NUT LOAF

1 1/2 cups boiling water
1 1/2 cups chopped dates
1 1/4 cups sugar
1 egg
2 tsp. baking soda

1/2 tsp. salt
1 tsp. vanilla
1 tbs. melted butter
2 1/2 cups flour
1 cup walnuts, chopped

In large bowl, pour boiling water over dates. Let stand 5 to 10 minutes. Stir in sugar, egg, baking soda, salt, vanilla, and butter. In small bowl, mix flour with nuts; stir into date mixture. Pour into two greased 1-lb. coffee cans or one 8-cup mold. Cover with foil and tie. Place cans or mold on rack in slow-cooking pot. Pour 2 cups hot water around cans. Cover pot and cook on high for 2 1/2 to 3 hours or until done. Remove from pot. Let bread stand in coffee cans 10 minutes; turn out onto cooling rack. Slice and spread with butter, cream cheese, or peanut butter.

PUMPKIN NUT BREAD

1 1/2 cups flour
1 1/4 tsp. soda
1 tsp. salt
1 tsp. ground cinnamon
1/2 tsp. ground nutmeg
1 cup canned pumpkin

1 cup sugar
1/2 cup buttermilk
1 egg
2 tbs. soft butter
1 cup chopped pecans

Sift flour, soda, salt, and spices. Combine pumpkin, sugar, buttermilk, and egg in mixing bowl. Add dry ingredients and butter; beat until well blended. Stir in nuts. Spread in well-greased and floured 4 to 5-cup mold or 1-lb. coffee can. Cover with foil. Place rack in slow-cooking pot. Pour 2 cups hot water in pot. Place covered bread container on rack. Cover pot and cook on high 3 to 4 hours. Turn out on cooling rack. Serve warm or cool.

PLUM PUDDING

4 slices bread, torn up
1 cup milk
2 slightly beaten eggs
1 cup light brown sugar
1/4 cup orange juice
6 oz. finely chopped suet (or ask butcher to
    grind it)
1 tsp. vanilla
1 cup flour

1 tsp. soda
1/2 tsp. salt
2 tsp. ground cinnamon
1 tsp. ground cloves
1 tsp. ground mace
2 cups raisins
1 cup pitted dates, cut up
1/2 cup chopped, mixed candied fruits and peels
1/2 cup coarsely chopped walnuts

Soak bread in milk; beat. Stir in eggs, sugar, juice, suet, and vanilla. In large bowl, combine flour with soda, salt, and spices. Add fruits and nuts. Mix well. Stir in bread mixture. Pour into well-greased 2-qt. mold. Cover with foil; tie with string. Place on metal rack or trivet in slow-cooking pot with 1 inch water. Cover pot and cook on high for 5 to 6 hours. Cool in pan 10 minutes; unmold. Serve warm, plain, or with hard sauce. Makes 10 to 12 servings.

Plum Pudding   Courtesy California Raisin Advisory Board

CHOCOLATE PUDDING CAKE

2 cups flour
2 tsp. baking powder
1/4 tsp. salt
1/2 cup cocoa powder
1/2 cup butter

1/2 cup sugar
4 eggs
1 cup milk
1 1/2 cups fresh bread crumbs
Chocolate or fudge sauce

Grease 1 1/2-qt. mold or baking dish. Sift flour, baking powder, salt, and cocoa. In large mixing bowl, cream butter and sugar; add eggs, one at a time, alternately with half the flour mixture. Beat well after each addition. Add milk alternately with remaining flour. Stir in bread crumbs. Pour into greased mold; cover with foil; tie. Place rack in slow-cooking pot. Add 2 cups hot water. Place mold with cake mixture on rack in pot. Cook, covered, on high for 3 to 4 hours. Serve warm or cold. To serve, slice cake and spoon chocolate or fudge topping over; top with whipped cream, if desired.

CARROT COFFEE CAKE

2 eggs
1 cup sugar
3/4 cup salad oil
1 1/2 cups flour
1 tsp. baking powder

3/4 tsp. baking soda
1/8 tsp. salt
1 tsp. cinnamon
1 cup finely shredded raw carrots

Beat eggs; add sugar gradually, beating until slightly thickened. Add oil gradually and continue beating until thoroughly combined. Stir in flour, baking powder, soda, salt, and cinnamon until mixture is smooth. Stir in carrots until blended well. Pour into greased and floured 6-cup mold. Cover with foil and tie. Put trivet or metal rack in slow-cooking pot. Pour 2 cups hot water in pot. Place filled mold on trivet or metal rack. Cover pot; cook on high for 2 1/2 to 3 1/2 hours or until done. Remove from pot; let stand 5 minutes on cooling rack. Loosen edges with knife. Turn out on rack and cool. This coffee cake can be used as a bread or cake. Serve either warm with butter, or cool with thin coating of butter or cream cheese frosting.

BANANA NUT CAKE

1 (18 1/2-oz.) package yellow cake mix
1/8 tsp. baking soda
1 cup water

2 eggs
1 cup mashed bananas (2 medium bananas)
1/2 cup finely chopped walnuts

In large mixing bowl, combine cake mix and soda. Add water, eggs, and bananas. Beat 4 minutes on medium speed of electric mixer. Fold in nuts. Pour into greased and floured 2-qt. mold. Place on bottom of slow-cooking pot. Cover cake with 4 to 5 paper towels. Cover pot and cook on high for 2 to 3 hours. Invert on cooling rack. Serve plain, dusted with powdered sugar, or drizzled with a thin glaze.

Short-Cut Fruit Cake   Courtesy California Raisin Advisory Board

SHORT-CUT FRUIT CAKE

1 (14-oz.) package date bar mix
2/3 cup hot water
3 eggs
1/4 cup flour
3/4 tsp. baking powder
2 tbs. light molasses
1 tsp. cinnamon

1/4 tsp. nutmeg
1/4 tsp. allspice
1 cup chopped nuts
1 cup raisins
1 (8-oz.) package candied red and green
    cherries

Grease and flour 6-cup ring mold. In large bowl, stir together date filling from date bar mix and water. Mix in dry crumbly mix, eggs, flour, baking powder, molasses, and spices thoroughly. Fold in nuts, raisins, and cherries. Spoon into mold. Cover with foil. Place metal rack or trivet in slow-cooking pot. Add 2 cups hot water.* Place filled mold in pot. Cover and cook on high for 2 to 3 hours. Cool and slice.

*Add more water after first hour of cooking, if needed.

Breads & Cakes   159

APPLESAUCE SPICE CAKE

1 (1-lb. 3-oz.) package spice cake mix

1 (1-lb.) can applesauce

2 eggs

Browned Butter Frosting:

1/3 cup butter

3 cups sifted powdered sugar

1 1/2 tsp. vanilla

2 tbs. milk

In large mixing bowl, combine cake mix with applesauce and eggs. Blend for 1/2 minute. Then beat at medium speed 4 minutes. Pour into greased and floured 6-cup mold. Place in slow-cooking pot. Arrange several layers of paper towels on top of mold. Cover slow-cooking pot, leaving lid slightly ajar. Cook on high for 2 to 3 hours. Let stand 5 minutes. Turn out on cooling rack. Cool; cover with frosting.

Frosting:

Heat butter in saucepan over medium heat until a delicate light brown, being careful not to let it get deep brown. Remove from heat. Stir in sugar, vanilla, and milk. Beat with a wooden spoon until smooth, adding a few drops of milk if mixture is too thick. Spread over cooled cake.

BLUEBERRY COFFEE CAKE

2 cups flour

1 cup sugar

4 tsp. baking powder

1/8 tsp. salt

2 eggs, beaten

1/2 cup salad oil

1/4 cup milk

1 tsp. vanilla

2 cups fresh or thawed frozen blueberries, drained

Crumb Topping:

1/4 cup softened butter

1/2 cup sugar

1/3 cup flour

1/2 tsp. ground cinnamon

In mixing bowl combine flour, sugar, baking powder and salt. Add eggs, oil, milk and vanilla. Beat until smooth. Fold in blueberries. Pour into greased 2-quart mold. Combine crumb topping ingredients and sprinkle on top of batter. Place in slow-cooking pot. Cover mold with 4 or 5 paper towels. Cover pot and cook on high 3 to 4 hours. Cool on rack for 5 minutes. Remove from mold. Serve warm. This dense blueberry coffee cake tastes great and would be ideal for Sunday brunch. Makes 6 to 8 servings.

FRUITS & DESSERTS

You can make desserts in your slow cooker. Actually, several types of desserts are perfectly suited because the slow cooker brings out those good old-fashioned flavors. It's hard to beat the taste of a fruit compote prepared in a pot. Long cooking at very low temperatures blends the fruit flavors with the spices, wines or liqueurs.

Fresh or dried fruits may be used in many combinations, depending on what's available in your market. Dried fruits are especially good when fixed in a slow cooker. Many of the desserts in this section are reminiscent of Grandmother's day. They require that old-time simmering which the slow cooker does so well.

If you have never tried real homemade mincemeat, try my *Mincemeat* recipe. It is a variation of an old Pennsylvania Dutch mince pie. Don't be frightened by the long list of ingredients. Cut the recipe in half if you want to start off on a smaller scale.

Traditional *Apple Butter* is so easy to make in a slow cooker. In the past you had to stir it almost constantly to keep it from sticking and scorching. That was before electrical slow cookers with low and even temperatures.

And, you can "bake" custard in a slow cooker. With *Rice Pudding* or *Lemon Pudding* it is a good idea to turn the control to HIGH. The custardy mixture must be cooked on a trivet in hot water, so the trick is to cook it on HIGH.

Let me caution you that every baking container and mold will not fit all slow cookers. If you have a small cooker, you will have to use other molds or cut some of the recipes down to fit your pot. Measure your pot carefully, then take your tape measure with you when you shop for pans or molds.

APPLE PEANUT CRUMBLE

4 or 5 cooking apples, peeled and sliced
2/3 cup brown sugar, packed
1/2 cup flour
1/2 cup quick-cooking rolled oats

1/2 tsp. cinnamon
1/2 tsp. nutmeg
1/3 cup butter, softened
2 tbs. peanut butter

Place apple slices in slow-cooking pot. In medium bowl, combine sugar, flour, oats, cinnamon, and nutmeg. Mix in butter and peanut butter with pastry blender or fork. Sprinkle over apples. Cover pot and cook on low for 5 to 6 hours. Serve warm; plain, with ice cream or whipped cream. Makes 4 to 5 servings.

HOME-STYLE APPLESAUCE

8 to 10 medium cooking apples, peeled and
  diced
1/2 cup water

3/4 cup sugar
Cinnamon

In slow-cooking pot, combine apples and water. Cover and cook on low for 4 to 6 hours or until apples are very soft. Add sugar and cook on low another 30 minutes. Sprinkle with cinnamon at serving time. Makes about 4 cups.

Note: Applesauce will be slightly chunky. If smooth sauce is preferred, puree or sieve cooked apples.

TRADITIONAL APPLE BUTTER

12 to 14 cooking apples (about 16 cups
  chopped)
2 cups cider

2 cups sugar
1 tsp. ground cinnamon
1/4 tsp. ground cloves

Core and chop apples. (Do not peel.) Combine apples and cider in slow-cooking pot. Cover and cook on low for 10 to 12 hours or until apples are mushy. Puree in food mill or sieve. Return pureed mixture to pot; add sugar, cinnamon, and cloves. Cover and cook on low one hour. Will keep several weeks in the refrigerator. Or, if desired, pour into hot sterilized jars and seal, or pour into freezer containers and freeze. Makes about 8 cups.

Fresh Pears in Wine   Courtesy Wine Growers of California

FRESH PEARS IN WINE

6 small fresh pears
1 cup sauterne wine
1 cup sugar

1/2 cup water
1 tsp. minced crystallized ginger
2 tbs. lemon juice

Peel pears, leaving fruit whole with stems intact. Place upright in slow-cooking pot. Combine wine with sugar, water, ginger, and lemon juice. Pour over pears. Cover and cook on low 4 to 6 hours or until pears are tender. Chill and serve plain, with sour cream or whipped cream cheese. Makes 6 servings.

Baked Apples　　Photo: Josh Young

APPLE BROWN BETTY

4 cups small bread cubes (about 1/2-inch)
1/2 cup melted butter or margarine
1/2 tsp. ground cinnamon
1/4 tsp. ground nutmeg

1/8 tsp. salt
3/4 cup firmly packed brown sugar
4 cups chopped, peeled cooking apples

Mix bread cubes with butter, cinnamon, nutmeg, salt and brown sugar. Arrange in alternate layers with apples in slow-cooking pot. Cover and cook on high for 1 1/2 to 2 1/2 hours or until apples are tender. Serve warm with cream, hard sauce or ice cream. Makes 4 to 5 servings.

SPICY APPLESAUCE

8 to 10 medium apples (eating kind)
1/2 cup water
3/4 cup sugar

1 tsp. ground cinnamon
1/2 tsp. ground nutmeg
1 tsp. ground cloves

Cut apples into medium-size pieces; do not core or peel. Place in slow-cooking pot with all other ingredients. Cook on low 7 to 8 hours until apples are very soft. Strain through seive. Serve hot or cold. Makes about 4 cups.

BAKED APPLES

5 to 6 baking apples
1/2 cup raisins or chopped dates
1 cup brown sugar
1 cup boiling water

2 tbs. butter or margarine
1/2 tsp. ground cinnamon
1/4 tsp. ground nutmeg

Core apples and peel each about 1/4 way down. Arrange in slow-cooking pot. Fill centers with raisins or dates. Combine sugar, water, butter, cinnamon, and nutmeg. Pour over apples. Cover and cook on low 2 to 4 hours (depending on size and variety of apples). Serve warm or cool. Makes 5 to 6 servings.

DANISH APPLE PUDDING

1 1/3 cups finely crushed zwieback (14 slices)
1/2 cup melted butter or margarine
1/2 cup brown sugar, packed

1 tsp. cinnamon
1 (16-oz.) can applesauce
1/2 cup chilled whipping cream

Combine zwieback crumbs with melted butter, sugar and cinnamon. Spoon applesauce into 1-qt. souffle or baking dish. Top with crumb mixture. Place baking dish in slow-cooking pot. Cover pot and cook on low for 3 to 4 hours. Serve warm or chilled. Whip cream; spoon onto pudding. Makes 5 to 6 servings.

CARAMEL APPLES

2 (14-oz.) bags caramels
1/4 cup water

8 to 10 medium apples

In slow-cooking pot, combine caramels and water. Cover and cook on high for 1 to 1 1/2 hours, stirring frequently. Wash and dry apples. Insert stick into stem end of each apple. Turn control on low. Dip apple into hot caramel and turn to coat entire surface. Holding apple above pot, scrape off excess accumulation of caramel from bottom of apple. Place on greased wax paper to cool.

SLOW-COOKING CRANBERRIES

1 (16-oz.) package fresh cranberries
2 cups sugar

1/4 cup water

Combine cranberries with sugar and water in slow-cooking pot. Cover and cook on high 2 to 3 hours or until some of the cranberries have "popped." Makes about 4 cups. Serve with chicken or turkey.

ST. HELENA PEARS

6 fresh pears
1/2 cup raisins
1/4 cup brown sugar
1 tsp. grated lemon peel

1/4 cup brandy
1/2 cup sauterne wine
1/2 cup macaroon crumbs

Peel and core pears; cut into thin slices. Mix raisins with sugar and lemon peel. Arrange alternately with pear slices in slow-cooking pot. Pour brandy and wine over. Cover pot and cook on low for 4 to 6 hours. Spoon into serving dishes, allow to cool. Sprinkle with macaroons. Serve plain or topped with sour cream. Makes 6 servings.

Fruit Compote Courtesy Cling Peach Advisory Board and California Prune Advisory Board

HOLIDAY FRUIT COMPOTE

1/4 cup port wine
1 tbs. butter
1 1/4 cups sugar
1 tbs. grated lemon peel
1/8 tsp. cinnamon
1/8 tsp. nutmeg

4 medium apples, peeled and sliced
2 cups fresh cranberries
1/2 cup chopped pitted dates
1/3 cup chopped walnuts
Dairy sour cream or ice cream

In slow-cooking pot, combine wine, butter, sugar, lemon peel, and spices. Add apples and cranberries. Cover and cook on low for 4 to 6 hours. Stir in dates and walnuts. Serve warm or cold. Delicious with topping of sour cream or used as a sundae sauce for ice cream.

ORANGE-PRUNE COMPOTE

1 lb. dried prunes
3 cups water
2 (11-oz.) cans mandarin oranges, drained
1/3 cup sugar

1/4 cup Cointreau or Curacao
1/2 cup orange juice
2 bananas, sliced

Pit prunes; combine with water in slow-cooking pot. Cover and cook on low for 2 to 2 1/2 hours. Cool and drain. Combine with mandarin oranges, sugar, Cointreau, and orange juice. Let stand in refrigerator several hours. Just before serving, add bananas. Makes 8 to 10 servings.

APPLE-CRANBERRY COMPOTE

5 or 6 cooking apples, peeled and sliced
1 cup fresh cranberries
1 cup sugar
1/2 tsp. grated orange peel

1/2 cup water
1/4 cup port wine
Dairy sour cream

Arrange apple slices and cranberries in slow-cooking pot. Sprinkle sugar over fruit. Add orange peel, water and wine. Stir to mix ingredients. Cover and cook on low for 4 to 6 hours or until apples are tender. Serve warm fruits with the juices, topped with dab of sour cream. Makes 5 to 6 servings.

STEAMED CHOCOLATE DESSERT

1/4 cup butter or margarine
1 1/8 cups sugar
1 egg, well beaten
1 cup fine dry bread crumbs
3 tbs. flour
1 1/2 tsp. baking powder

1/4 tsp. salt
1/2 cup milk
2 squares unsweetened chocolate, melted
1/2 tsp. vanilla
1/4 cup chopped pecans

In large bowl, cream butter; add sugar gradually. Add eggs; mix until thick and fluffy. Combine dry bread crumbs, flour, baking powder and salt. Add milk, alternately with dry ingredients, to sugar-butter mixture beginning and ending with dry ingredients. Stir in melted chocolate, vanilla and pecans. Pour into greased 1-quart mold. Cover with foil; tie. Place on metal rack or trivet in slow-cooking pot. Pour 2 cups hot water around mold. Cover pot; cook on high for 2 to 3 hours. Spoon into bowls and serve with whipped cream or mint ice cream. Makes 4 to 6 servings.

CROCKERY-STEWED PRUNES

1 (1-lb.) package dried prunes
3 cups water

2 thin lemon slices

In slow-cooking pot, combine prunes with water and lemon slices. Cover and cook on low for 2 hours or until prunes are plump and tender. Serve warm or cold. Makes 6 to 8 servings.

FRUIT MEDLEY

1 1/2 lbs. mixed dried fruits
2 1/2 cups water
1 cup sugar
1 tbs. honey
Peel of 1/2 lemon, cut into thin strips

1/8 tsp. nutmeg
1 cinnamon stick
3 tbs. cornstarch
1/4 cup Cointreau

Put dried fruit into slow-cooking pot. Pour in water. Stir in sugar, honey, lemon peel, and spices. Cover and cook on low for 2 to 3 hours. Turn control to high. Mix cornstarch in small amount of water; stir into fruit mixture. Cook on high for 10 minutes or until thickened. Add Cointreau. Serve warm or chilled. May be served as fruit compote or as topping for ice cream. Makes 5 to 6 servings.

HOMEMADE MINCEMEAT

2 1/2 lbs. beef shanks
4 cups water
1/2 lb. beef suet
2 lbs. tart apples, peeled and diced
1 (15-oz.) package seedless raisins
1 (11-oz.) package currants
1 tbs. grated lemon peel
1 tbs. lemon juice
1 tbs. grated orange peel

1/4 cup orange juice
1 tsp. cinnamon
1/2 tsp. ground cloves
1/2 tsp. nutmeg
1 tsp. salt
1/2 cup molasses
1/2 cup brown sugar, packed
1 1/2 cups apple cider

Combine beef and water in slow-cooking pot. Cover and cook on low for 8 to 10 hours. Save all the broth; remove beef from bones. In food chopper, grind beef and suet together. Combine with 1/2 cup broth and remaining ingredients in slow-cooking pot. Cover and cook on low 8 to 10 hours. Makes 3 qts. mincemeat or enough for four 9-inch pies. In making pies, 2 or 3 tbs. brandy or bourbon may be added to filling for each pie. Filling can be kept in refrigerator for several days or frozen for about 6 months. Extra broth can be used for soup base.

DOWN-HOME RHUBARB

2 lbs. fresh rhubarb (about 7 to 8 cups)
1/2 cup water

1 1/2 cups sugar
1/2 tsp. vanilla (optional)

Trim rhubarb and cut into 1-inch pieces. Combine with water and sugar in slow-cooking pot. Cover and cook on low 2 to 3 hours. Add vanilla, if desired. Chill. Makes about 4 cups.

SPICED RHUBARB BAKE

1 1/2 lbs. fresh rhubarb
3/4 cup sugar
1 cinnamon stick
3 whole cloves

1 tsp. grated orange or lemon peel
1/4 cup butter or margarine
1/4 cup flour
1/3 cup sugar

Cut rhubarb into 1-inch pieces. In slow-cooking pot, combine rhubarb with 3/4 cup sugar, cinnamon, cloves, and grated peel. Cover and cook on low for 3 to 4 hours. Remove cinnamon and cloves. Spoon rhubarb into shallow baking dish. In small bowl, mix together butter, flour and 1/3 cup sugar with fork or pastry blender. Sprinkle over cooked rhubarb. Bake in 400°F. oven for about 20 minutes. Makes 5 to 6 servings.

LEMON PUDDING CAKE

3 eggs, separated
1 tsp. grated lemon peel
1/4 cup lemon juice
3 tbs. butter

1 1/2 cups milk
3/4 cup sugar
1/4 cup flour
1/8 tsp. salt

Beat egg whites until stiff peaks form; set aside. Beat egg yolks; blend in lemon peel, juice, butter, and milk. Combine sugar, flour, and salt; add to egg-milk mixture, beating until smooth. Fold into beaten whites. Spoon into slow-cooking pot. Cover and cook on high for 2 to 3 hours. Makes 5 to 6 servings.

HOME-STYLE BREAD PUDDING

2 eggs, slightly beaten
2 1/4 cups milk
1 tsp. vanilla
1/2 tsp. ground cinnamon

1/4 tsp. salt
2 cups 1-inch bread cubes
1/2 cup brown sugar
1/2 cup raisins or chopped dates

In medium mixing bowl, combine eggs with milk, vanilla, cinnamon, salt, bread, sugar, and raisins or dates. Pour into 1 1/2-qt. baking dish. Place metal trivet or rack in bottom of slow-cooking pot. Add 1/2 cup hot water. Set baking dish on trivet. Cover pot; cook on high for about 2 hours. Serve pudding warm or cool. Makes 4 to 6 servings.

Rice Pudding　　　　Courtesy California Raisin Advisory Board

RICE PUDDING

1 cup uncooked regular rice
3 cups milk
3 tbs. butter
1/2 tsp. salt
1/2 cup sugar

3 eggs, beaten
1 tsp. vanilla
1 cup raisins
Cinnamon

Cook rice according to package directions. Combine cooked rice with milk, butter, salt, sugar, eggs, vanilla, and raisins. Pour into 1 1/2-qt. baking dish. Sprinkle with cinnamon. Cover baking dish with foil, not plastic. Place on metal trivet or rack in bottom of slow-cooking pot. Add 1 cup hot water to pot. Cover and cook on high for 2 hours. Makes 6 to 8 servings.

FAVORITE BAKED CUSTARD

2 cups milk, scalded
3 eggs, slightly beaten
1/3 cup sugar

1 tsp. vanilla
1/8 tsp. salt
Nutmeg or coconut

Scald milk, let cool slightly. Combine eggs, sugar, vanilla, and salt. Slowly stir in slightly cooled milk. Pour into buttered 1-qt. baking dish. Sprinkle with nutmeg or coconut. Cover with foil. Set baking dish on metal rack or trivet in slow-cooking pot. Pour hot water around baking dish, 1 inch deep. Cover pot and cook on high for 2 to 2 1/2 hours or until knife inserted in custard comes out clean. Serve warm or chilled. Makes 5 to 6 servings.

CHOCOLATE FONDUE

6 (1-oz.) squares unsweetened chocolate
1 1/2 cups sugar
1 cup light cream
1/2 cup butter or margarine
1/8 tsp. salt

3 tbs. creme de cacao or coffee-flavored liqueur
Angel cake cut into bite-size chunks
Marshmallows
Fruits (such as bananas, strawberries, maraschino
   cherries, or pineapple)

Place chocolate in slow-cooking pot. Cover and heat on high for about 30 minutes or until chocolate melts. Stir in sugar, cream, butter, and salt. Cook on high, stirring constantly, for about 10 minutes or until blended. Add creme de cacao. Turn control to low. Spear angel cake chunks, marshmallows or fruits with fondue fork. Dip into chocolate mixture. Keep chocolate hot in slow-cooking pot. Makes about 6 to 8 servings.

MINT WAFERS

2 tbs. butter
1/4 cup milk
1 package (about 15 oz.) white creamy frosting mix

Several drops mint flavoring
Food coloring (optional)

Combine butter and milk in slow-cooking pot. Turn control to high; cover and heat until butter melts. Stir in frosting mix. Cook on high for 1 to 2 minutes, stirring occasionally. Add flavoring and color, if desired. Turn to low. Drop from teaspoon onto waxed paper, swirling tips with spoon. Keep slow-cooking pot control on low while forming patties. If candy gets too thick, add several drops hot water. Makes 5 dozen.

MILK CHOCOLATE SAUCE

1 (16-oz.) milk chocolate candy bar   1/3 cup butter
1 cup light cream   1 tsp. vanilla

In slow-cooking pot, break chocolate into small pieces. Add cream and butter. Cover and cook on low for 2 to 2 1/2 hours or until chocolate melts. Stir in vanilla. Beat until smooth. Serve warm over pound cake, angel cake, or ice cream. Makes about 3 cups sauce.

ROSY FRUIT TOPPING

1 (20-oz.) can pineapple chunks   1 tsp. grated lemon peel
1 (29-oz.) can sliced cling peaches   1/2 cup peach brandy, heated
3 tbs. butter   Vanilla ice cream
1/2 cup currant jelly

Drain pineapple and peaches. Combine fruit with butter, jelly, and lemon peel in slow-cooking pot. Cover and cook on low for 2 to 3 hours. Stir in warm brandy. Spoon over ice cream. Makes 8 servings.

INDEX

A

Acorn Squash, Indonesian, 104
All-American Snack, 113
All-Purpose Barbecue Sauce, 76
Almonds, 113
Alphabet Pot Roast, 48
Alphabet Soup, 124
Altitudes, high, 5, 142
Aluminum, care of, 8
Aluminum foil, 6, 151-152
Americanized Chicken Chop Suey, 86
Anne's Chicken, 90
Appetizer Ribs, 112
Appetizers, 111-115
Apple Brandy Brew, 120
Apple Brown Betty, 165
Apple Butter, 162
Apple-Cranberry Compote, 168
Apple Peanut Crumble, 162
Apples, 160, 162, 165-166
Applesauce Spice Cake, 160
Apricot Punch, Spiced, 120
Arroz Con Pollo, 84
Auto-Shift, 13, 16
Autumn Pork Chops, 69

B

Baked Apples, 165
Baked Bean Cassoulet, 146
Baked Bean Soup, 143
Baked enamel, care of, 8
Baking, 11, 150-160
Banana Nut Bread, 155
Banana Nut Cake, 158
Barbecue Beef Sandwiches, 134
Barbecue Sauce, All-Purpose, 76
Barbecued Beef & Beans, 42
Barbecued Spareribs, 76
Barbecued Turkey Legs, 91
Bean Soup, 143
Beans, 42, 44, 115, 142-148
    Barbecued Beef &, 42
    Cooking, 142
    Dip, 115
    Southwestern Beef &, 44
Beef, 28-66, 123-124, 127, 131, 134, 139, 147
    Brisket, 55
    Corned, 52
    Directions for slow-cooking, 28
    Ground, 55, 57-66, 134, 139, 147
    Liver, 44
    Roasts, 48-50, 56
    Short ribs, 44, 46-47, 127
    Steak
        Chuck, 37
        Flank, 37-40
        Round, 29-35, 41
    Stew meat, 41-44, 123
    Stroganoff, 32, 61
    Tongue, 52
Beef Burgundy, 41
Beef Shank Soup, 131
Beefburger Stroganoff, 61
Beets, 99
Beverages, 111, 116-121
Bishop's Wine, 117

Black Eyed Peas, Mexican Style, 148
Blueberry Coffee Cake, 160
Boston Baked Beans, 145
Boston Brown Bread, 154
Bouillabaise, 132
Breads, 150-156
Brisket, 55
Browning units, 6
Brunswick Stew, 91
Buck's County Spareribs, 76
Budget Beef Stroganoff, 32
Burgundy-Basted Duckling, 97
Busy Woman's Roast Chicken, 86
Buttered Punch, Hot, 117

C

Cabbage, 63, 79, 100, 125
Cabbage Rolls, 63
    How to stuff, 63
Cabbage Soup, Swedish, 125
Cakes, 150, 153, 158-160, 170
California Tamale Pie, 140
Candied Yams & Cranberries, 107
Caramel Apples, 166
Care of slow-cooking pots, 5-9
Carrot Coffee Cake, 158
Carrots, 99-101
Carrots in Dilled Wine Sauce, 101
Cassoulet en Pot, 78
Cauliflower Soup, Cream of, 128
Celery, 99
Cheese, 114-115, 135, 136, 141
Cheese Fondue, 141
Cheesy Meat Loaf, 64
Chicken, 78, 80-91, 113, 114, 133
    Directions for slow cooking, 80
    Livers, 114
Chicken & Herb Dumplings, 90
Chicken Breasts, Saltimbocca Style, 87
Chicken Cacciatora, 89
Chicken Kona, 82
Chicken Marengo, 81
Chicken Napoli, 88
Chicken Olé, 84
Chicken Parmigiana, 87
Chicken Salad, Hot, 133
Chicken Sesame, 82
Chicken Tetrazzini, 88
Chili con Carne, 66
Chili con Queso, 115
Chili Dogs, 133
Chili Nuts, 113
Chili Relleno, Mock, 139
Chinese Beef and Pea Pods, 36
Chinese Pepper Steak, 35
Chinese Style Country Ribs, 73
Chocolate Dessert, Steamed, 168
Chocolate Fondue, 172
Chocolate Pudding Cake, 158
Chop Suey, 86
Chuck, 35
Chutney, 103
Cider, Mulled, 117
Clam Chowder, New England, 132
Clara's Beef & Potatoes, 61
Claret, Hot Spiced, 116
Cleaning, 8-9
Coffee Cakes, 158, 160
Coffee, Mediterranean, 116
Compotes, 167-169
Congressional Bean Soup, 143
Consumers' Guide to Slow-Cooking Pots, 10-27
Continental Cooker, 16

Conversion Chart, Metric, 9
Cooking times, 4, 5, 6, 11-27
Cornbread, 140
Corn Chowder, 125
Corn Pudding, 101
Corn-Stuffed Pork Chops, 71
Corn Stuffing Balls, 101
Corned Beef, 52, 134
Corning Electromatic Table Range, 11
Corning Ware, care of, 9
Cornish Hens, 94-95
Cornwall Crockery Cooker, 11, 153
Cornwall Tray Model Crockery Cookers, 12, 13
Cranberries, 72, 93, 107, 120, 155, 166, 168
Cranberry Nut Bread, 155
Cranberry Pork Roast, 72
Cran-Orange Turkey Roll, 93
Cream of Cauliflower Soup, 128
Create 'n Serve, 19
Creole Chicken, 84
Creole Steak Strips, 29
Creole Zucchini, 108
Crock-A-Dial, 13, 153
Crockery, care of, 8
Crockery Cooker, 11, 22, 153
Crockery Cookpot, 15, 153
Crockery Ham, 77
Crockery-Stewed Prunes, 169
Crock-Pots, 21, 153
Crock-Watcher 16, 153
Curried Almonds, 113
Curried Chicken, 83
Custard, 172

D

Dad's Ham & Potatoes, 141
Danish Apple Pudding, 166
Date and Nut Loaf, 156
Desserts, 161-173
Dilled Pot Roast, 50
Dips, 114-115
Dominion Crock-A-Dial & Crock-A-Dial II, 13, 153
Double Squash Combo, 105
Down East Corn Chowder, 125
Down-Home Rhubarb, 170
Drinks, 111, 116-121
Duckling, 80, 96-98

E

East Indian Snack, 114
Empire Easy Meal Slow Cooker, 14
Enamel, baked, care of, 8
Extension cords, 7

F

Family Favorite Meat Loaf, 65
Farberware Pot-Pourri, 14, 153
Farm Style Stew, 41
Favorite Baked Custard, 172
Favorite Pot Roast, 48
Festive Meat Balls, 60
Finger Drumsticks, 113
Flank Steak Creole, 37
Flank Steak in Mushroom Sauce
Flank Steak, Stuffed, 38
Flemish Carbonades, 35
Foil, aluminum, 6, 151, 152
Fondue, 57, 114, 141, 172
Fondue Italiano, 57
Frankfurters, 133
French Onion Soup, 127

Fresh Pears in Wine, 163
Frozen foods, 6
Fruit cake, 159
Fruit compote, 167
Fruit Medley, 169
Fruited Flank Steak, 40
Fruited Pork Chops, 70
Fruits, 161-170

G

Georgia Peanut Soup, 125
German Short Ribs, 47
Ginger Brown Bread, 154
Glass liners, care of, 9
Glazed Corned Beef, 52
Golden Glow Pork Chops, 69
Golden West Duckling, 97
Goulash, 47
Gourmet Leg of Lamb, 68
Grandinetti All-American Crockery Casserole, 15
Grandinetti Crockery Cook Pots, 15, 16, 1
Green Beans Portuguese Style, 102
Green Peppers, Stuffed, 64
Green Vegetable Chowder, 129
Ground beef, 55, 57-66, 134, 139, 147

H

Ham, 77, 78, 135, 141, 146
Ham and Chicken Pie, 78
Ham-Stuffed French Rolls, 122, 135
Hamburger, 55, 57-66, 134, 139, 147
Hamburger Soup, 61
Hamilton Beach Continental Cooker, Crock-Watcher and Simmer-On, 16
Hearty Alphabet Soup, 124
Herbed Leg of Lamb, 68
Herbed Pork Roast, 72
Herbed Spinach Soup, 129
Herbed Squash au Gratin, 105
High altitudes, 5, 142
Holiday Fruit Compote, 167
Home-Style Applesauce, 162
Home-Style Bread Pudding, 170
Home-Style Short Ribs, 46
Home-Style Tomato Juice, 112
Homemade Mincemeat, 169
Homestead Ham Loaf, 78
Hot Buttered Punch, 117
Hot Chicken Salad, 133
Hot Mint Malt, 121
Hot Spiced Claret, 116
Hot Spicy Lemonade Punch, 120
Hot Wine Cranberry Punch, 120
Hungarian Goulash, 47

I

Imperial Duckling, 98
Indonesian Pork, 73
Intermatic Timers, 6, 7
Irish Lamb Stew, 69
Italian Beef & Potato Casserole, 64
Italian Meat Ball Stew, 57
Italian Pot Roast, 56
Italian Vegetable Soup, 124

J

Jambalaya, 137

K

K-Mart LaCuisine SimRpot, 24
Knockwurst & Cabbage, 79
Knockwurst with Hot German Potato Salad, 79
Kowloon Chicken, 82

L

Lamb, 68-69
    Directions for slow cooking, 67
Lasagne, 55
Lazy Day Slo-Cooker, 27
Lemon Pudding Cake, 170
Lemonade Punch, Hot Spicy, 120
Lentil Soup—Crescenti Style, 131
Lima beans, 145, 147-148
Lime-Glazed Cornish Hens, 95
Liver, 44, 114
Liver Pate Bon Appetit, 114

M

Mac's Kidney Beans, 148
Marco Polo Short Ribs, 44
Mardi Gras Pot O' Plenty, 19
Measurements, Table of, 9
Meat Ball Stew, Italian, 57
Meat Balls, Festive, 60
Meat Loaf, 64, 65
Meat rack, 6, 8
Mediterranean Coffee, 116
Menu-planning guide, 4-5
Metric Conversion Chart, 9
Mexican Beef, 29
Mexican Style Short Ribs, 47
Milk Chocolate Sauce, 173
Mincemeat, 169
Minestrone Soup, 127
Mint Malt, Hot, 121
Mint Wafers, 172
Mission Chicken, 81
Mixed Vegetables en Pot, 110
Mock Chili Relleno, 139
Moist Cornbread, 140
Molasses Bread, 154
Molds, 153
Mother-in-Law's Sauerkraut, 100
Mulled Cider, 117

N

Nesco Pot Luck Cooker, 17, 153
New England Chuck Roast, 35
New England Clam Chowder, 132
North-of-the-Border Pozole, 72
No-Stick, care of, 13
Nut breads, 155-156
Nuts, 113-114
Nutty Chicken Breast, 86

O

Old Fashioned Beef Stew, 42
Old Fashioned Vegetable Soup, 127
Old World Sauerbraten, 48
Onion Soup, French, 127
Orange-Glazed Carrots, 100
Orange-Glazed Parsnips, 103
Orange-Prune Compote, 168
Oster Super Pot, 17, 153
Overstuffed Tuna-Egg Salad Rolls, 122, 132
Oxtail Stew, 42

P

Padre Punch, 117
Paella in a Pot, 138
Pans, baking, 153
Parsnips, 99, 103
Pasta, 136
Peach Chutney, 103
Peanut Butter Loaf, 155
Peanut Soup, 125
Pears, 163, 166
Penneys Slow Cooker/Fryer, 18, 153

Pennys Slow Crockery Cooker, 18
Pizza Beans, 146
Plantation Pork Chops, 71
Plum Pudding, 156
Poached Chicken, 90
Porcelain, care of, 8
Pork, 67, 69-79, 112, 135, 141, 146
    Chops, 69, 71
        How to stuff, 71
    Directions for slow cooking, 67
    Ham, 77-78, 135, 141, 146
    Roasts, 72-73
    Spareribs, 73-76, 112
    Steaks, 72
Portuguese Bean Soup, 143
Pot Luck Cooker, 17, 153
Pot O' Plenty, 19, 153
Pot-Pourri, 14, 153
Potatoes, 99, 103, 141
    Baked, 99
Poultry, 80-98
Pound Cake, 153
Pozole, North-of-the-Border, 72
Presto Slow Cookers, 19, 153
Prunes, 168, 169
Puddings, 156-158, 170-171
Pumpkin Nut Bread, 156
Punch, 111, 116-121

R

Ranch Style Beans, 146
Ranch Style Beef, 41
Rathskeller Pork, 72
Red Raisin Cornish Hens, 95
Refried Bean Dip, 115
Regal Mardi Gras Pot O' Plenty, 19, 153
Regal Poly Pot, 20
Reliable Crockery Slow Cooker, 20
Reuben Sandwiches, 134
Rhineland Sweet-Sour Red Cabbage, 100
Rhubarb, 170
Ribs; see Beef, Short ribs and Pork, Spareribs
Rice, 136
Rice Pudding, 171
Rival Crock-Pots, 21, 153
Roasts; see Beef, Pork or Turkey
Robeson SimRpot, 24
Rosy Fruit Topping, 173
Round Steak Italiano, 31
Round Steak with Rich Gravy, 31
Round Steak; also see Beef, Steak

S

St. Helena Pears, 166
Sandwiches, 132-135
Sauces
    All-Purpose Barbecue, 76
    Milk Chocolate, 173
    Rosy Fruit Topping, 173
Sauerbraten, 48
Sauerkraut, 100, 134
Sausage, 78-80, 107
Sausage-Stuffed Yams, 107
Savory Tomato Limas, 147
Sears Create 'n Serve Pan, 19
Sears Crockery Cookers, 22, 153
Shell Casserole, 138
Short-Cut Chili Con Carne, 66
Short-Cut Fondue Dip, 114
Short-Cut Fruit Cake, 159
Short-Cut Italian Vegatable Soup, 124
Short ribs 44, 46-47, 127
Shrimp Marinara, 138

Shrimp, shelling, 137
Simmer-On, 21, 153
Simpsons (Sears) Crockery Cooker, 22, 153
Sim-R-Ware, 24
Sloppy Jane Sandwiches, 133
Sloppy Joes, 134
Slow Cookery Sweet Potatoes, 108
Slow-Cooking Cranberries, 166
Smoky Brisket, 55
Snacks, 113-114
Soups, 122-132, 143
Sour Cream Limas, 145
Southwestern Beef & Beans, 44
Southwestern Ham & Beans, 146
Soy-Glazed Spareribs, 75
Spaghetti Sauce, 57
Spaghetti, Vegetarian, 140
Spanish Style Liver, 44
Spareribs, 73-76, 112
Spiced Apricot Punch, 120
Spiced Beef Tongue, 52
Spiced Rhubarb Bake, 170
Spices, 8, 176
Spice Chart, 176
Spicy Applesauce, 165
Spicy Brisket, 55
Spicy Lamb Shanks, 68
Spicy Tomato Juice Cocktail, 112
Spicy Wine Pot Roast, 49
Spinach Soup, Herbed, 129
Split Pea Soup, 131
Squash, 69, 104-105, 108, 109
Squash Medley, 105
St. Helena Pears, 166
Stainless steel, care of, 8
Steak; see Beef, Steak
Steamed Chocolate Dessert, 168
Steamed Molasses Bread, 154
Stewed Tomatoes, 110
Stews, 41-43
Stroganoff, 32, 61
Stuffed Butternut Squash, 104
Stuffed Flank Steak, 38
Stuffed Green Peppers, 64
Stuffed Honeyed Sweet Potatoes, 108
Stuffed Pattypan Squash, 105
Stuffed Potatoes, 103
Stuffed Turkey Breast, 92
Sunbeam Crocker Cooker Fryer, 23, 153
Sunbeam Crockery Frypan, 23
Super Pot, 17, 153
Swedish Cabbage Rolls, 63
Swedish Cabbage Soup, 125
Swedish Style Steak, 33
Sweet & Sour Turkey Wings, 94
Sweet potatoes, 99, 107-108
Sweet-Sour Bean Trio, 147
Sweet-Sour Spareribs, 73
Swiss Beef Birds, 33
Swiss Steak, 33

T

Table of Measurements, 9
Tamale pie, 140
Tamale Puff, 102
Tavern Soup, 129
Tea, 116
Teflon, care of, 9
Temperature control units, 6
Temperatures, 5-6, 10-27
Teriyaki Steak, 37
Thermostatic-heat-control unit, 6
Timers, 6

Tomato juice, 112
Tomatoes, 110
Tongue, 52
Tortilla Pie, 139
Traditional Apple Butter, 162
Trivets, 6, 7
Tropical Tea Warmer, 116
Tuna-Egg Salad Rolls, 132
Turkey, 91-95
    Breast, how to stuff, 92
    Directions for slow cooking, 80
Turkey Loaf, 95
Turkey Noodle Soup, 124
Turnip Whip, 102
Turnips, 99, 102

U

Use and care of slow-cooking pots, 5-9

V

Van Wyck SimRpot, 24
Van Wyck Sim-R-Ware, 24
Vegetable soup, 127
Vegetarian Spaghetti, 140
Vermont Baked Beans with Ham, 145

W

Wards Crockery Slow Cooker, 25
Wards Sim-R-Ware, 24
Wear·Ever Pokey·Pot, 25
Welsh Rarebit, 135
West Bend Colonial Crock Slo-Cooker and Beans 'N Stuff Slo-Cooker, 26
West Bend 4 Qt. Slo-Cooker, 26
West Bend Lazy Day Slo-Cooker, 27
West Bend Slo-Cooker Plus™ Automatic Cooker, 27
Wines, 116-120
Winter Warm-Up, 116

Y

Yam Pudding, 107
Yams, 99, 107-108

Z

Zippy Beans and Hominy, 147
Zippy Tomato Appetizer, 112
Zucchini, 108-109
Zucchini Casserole, 109

Order *Crockery Cookery* ($4.95 paperback, $6.95 hardback) from your bookstore or department store or direct from H. P. Books, Box 5367 Tucson, AZ 85703 602/888-2150 Include 50¢ for postage and handling. Allow 3 to 4 weeks for delivery.

SPICE CHART

NAME AND DESCRIPTION	COMPATIBLE WITH:
Allspice Color—brown Flavor—spicy, sweet, mild, pleasant	All cranberry dishes, spice cakes, beef stew, baked ham, mincemeat and pumpkin pie, tapioca & chocolate pudding
Anise Color—brown with tan stripes Flavor—sweet licorice aroma and taste	Coffee cake, rolls, cookies, all fruit pie fillings, sweet pickles, stewed fruits
Basil Color—light green Flavor—mild, sweet	All tomato dishes, green vegetables, stews, shrimp and lobster dishes
Bay Leaves Color—light green Flavor—very mild, sweet	Vegetables, stews, shrimp, lobster, chicken dishes, pot roasts
Caraway Color—dark brown with light brown stripes Flavor—like rye bread	Cheese spreads, breads and rolls, cookies, vegetables, roast pork
Cardamom Color—cream-colored pod, dark brown seeds Flavor—bitter-sweet	Danish pastry, coffee cake, custards, sweet potato and pumpkin dishes
Cayenne Color—burnt orange Flavor—hot	Deviled eggs, fish dishes, cooked green vegetables, cheese souffles, pork chops, veal stew
Celery Seed Color—shades of brownish green Flavor—bitter celery	Meat loaf, fish chowders, cole slaw, stewed tomatoes, rolls, salad dressings
Chili Powder Color—light to dark red Flavor—distinctive, hot	Mexican cookery, chili, beef, pork and veal dishes, Spanish rice
Cinnamon Color—light brown Flavor—sweet and spicy	Coffee cakes, spice cake, cookies, puddings, fruit pies, spiced beverages, sweet potato and pumpkin dishes
Cloves Color—dark brown Flavor—spicy, sweet, pungent	Ham, apple, mince & pumpkin pies, baked beans, hot tea, spice cake, puddings, cream of pea and tomato soups
Cumin Color—gold with a hint of green Flavor—salty sweet	Deviled eggs, chili, rice, fish
Curry Powder Color—Predominantly rich gold Flavor—exotic with heat	Eggs, fish, poultry, creamed vegetables, chowders, tomato soup, salted nuts
Dill Color—greenish brown Flavor—similar to caraway, but milder and sweeter	Pickling, potato salad, soups, vegetables, salad dressing, drawn butter for shellfish
Ginger Color—tan Flavor—spicy	Cookies, spice cake, pumpkin pie, puddings, applesauce, stews, French dressing

NAME AND DESCRIPTION	COMPATIBLE WITH:
Mace Color—burnt orange Flavor—similar to nutmeg, exotic	Fish, stews, pickling, gingerbread, cakes. Welsh rarebit, chocolate dishes, fruit pies
Marjoram Color—green Flavor—delicate	Lamb chops, roast beef, poultry, omelets, stews, stuffings
Mint Color—green Flavor—sweet	Jelly, fruit salad, lamb and veal roast, tea
Mustard Color—light to dark brown Flavor—spicy, sharp	Pickling, Chinese hot sauce, cheese sauce, vegetables, molasses cookies
Nutmeg Color—copper Flavor—exotic, sweet	Doughnuts, eggnog, custards, spice cake, coffee cake, pumpkin pie, sweet potatoes
Oregano Color—green Flavor—strong	Pizza, spaghetti sauce, meat sauces, soups, vegetables
Paprika Color—red Flavor—very mild	Poultry, goulash, vegetables, canapes, chowders
Parsley Color—green Flavor—mild	Soups, salads, meat stews, all vegetables, potatoes
Pepper Color—black or white Flavor—spicy, enduring aftertaste	Almost all foods except those with sweet flavors. Use white pepper when black specks are not desired.
Poppy Seeds Color—blue-gray Flavor—crunchy, nutlike	Breads and rolls, salad dressings, green peas
Rosemary Color—green Flavor—delicate, sweetish	Lamb, beef, pork, poultry, soups, cheese sauces, potatoes
Saffron Color—red-orange Flavor—exotic	Rice, breads, fish stew, chicken soup, cakes
Savory Color—green Flavor—mild, pleasant	Scrambled eggs, poultry stuffing, hamburgers, fish, tossed salad
Sesame Seeds Color—cream Flavor—crunchy, nutlike	Breads and rolls, cookies, salad dressings, fish, asparagus
Tarragon Color—green Flavor—fresh, pleasant	Marinades of meat, poultry, omelets, fish, soups, vegetables
Thyme Color—olive green Flavor—pleasantly penetrating	Tomato dishes, fish chowder, all meats, potatoes
Tumeric Color—orange Flavor—mild, slightly bitter	Pickles, salad dressings, seafood, rice

25.9129897282